CW00970057

RADIO
JOURNALISM
TOOLKIT

Franz Krüger

OPEN SOCIETY FOUNDATION
FOR SOUTH AFRICA

publishers

Published by the Institute for the Advancement
of Journalism and STE Publishers

First published in 2006 by
Institute for the Advancement of Journalism (IAJ)
9 Jubilee Road
Parktown 2193
Johannesburg
and
STE Publishers
4th Floor Sunnyside Ridge,
Sunnyside Office Park,
32 Princess of Wales Terrace,
Parktown 2143
Johannesburg, South Africa

ISBN 1-919855-79-3

Acknowledgements

Text Editor:	Jo-Anne Richards
Photographs	Franz Krüger, PictureNet, IAJ and NCRF
Book design:	Adam Rumball, Mad Cow Studio,
	a division of STE Publishers
CD-ROM:	Fuad Vally, Best Boy Productions,
	a division of Burn Masters
Printing:	Clickrite

Contents

Foreword

Radio journalism is, to me, the most critical of all forms of journalism.
Print journalism can be read over and over again to make sense of the stories,
and there are images to support the written word in telling the story. Television
journalism is the most privileged form of journalism, combining voice and visu-
als with text to tell the story.

Radio journalism only has the spoken word. Sometimes it is seen as a less
serious form of journalism than print and TV. And yet it has enormous
strengths. It is immediate, and the human voice has tremendous power to
evoke images, and take listeners to the scene.

Radio journalists have a particular responsibility in Africa since millions of
people rely on radio for their information. In recognition of the importance
of the medium, the IAJ is committed to supporting programmes for the
improvement of radio journalism, and is happy to introduce this Radio
Journalism Toolkit.

It is targeted at institutions of higher learning, as well as service providers who
offer short courses and longer skills programmes (as institutions and freelance
trainers), and in-house radio newsroom trainers.

The South African Qualifications Authority (SAQA) and National Qualifications
Framework (NQF) processes have been daunting for both the journalism
industry and trainers. This toolkit attempts to simplify the processes towards a
radio journalism component in the SAQA Journalism Qualification.

We hope that radio journalists themselves will find this toolkit a user-friendly guide, and that it will help improve knowledge and skills in the field generally.

This toolkit is very practical. It is full of exercises and practical tips. A unique feature is that it includes a CD with audio material to practice on and other material.

The author, Franz Krüger has extensive experience in broadcast and print journalism, in both the mainstream and community sectors. His approach to teaching radio journalism takes into account the needs of students at tertiary institutions, as well as working journalists across the sectors. The IAJ could not have chosen a better author.

The institute is indebted to the Open Society Foundation for South Africa (OSF-SA) for the financial support that helped make this Toolkit a reality.

Leli elinye lamagalelo e IAJ (another IAJ effort) to make practical journalism better.

Jacob Ntshangase
IAJ Executive Director
2006

Introduction

Welcome to The Radio Journalism Toolkit. It is intended as a resource for students, community radio journalists, trainers – anyone who cares about journalism on radio.

The medium of radio is the only source of information for many people. It has many advantages that allow it to reach much deeper into communities than TV, print and the Internet. Even people who have access to other sources of information still keep space in their lives for the humble radio.

These millions of listeners deserve reliable and professionally produced journalism. Radio journalists have a responsibility to do their work as well as they possibly can.

It is a very varied sector. There are tightly controlled state broadcasters and public broadcasters who try to serve the public; there are commercial stations who rake in money for their owners and community stations who can hardly pay the rent. Some stations have large organisations and the latest equipment – others have almost nothing, relying on the generosity of volunteers and donors.

The toolkit tries to take into account the range of situations radio journalists may find themselves in. There are stations that produce only bulletins, and whose primary concern is the ability to turn soundbites around quickly. Others make space for sound-rich packages, and require a different set of skills. This toolkit will cover both areas – and more, since a well-rounded radio journalist needs to fit into different news set-ups.

The toolkit has been written to fit in with the journalism qualification accepted by the SA Qualifications Authority (SAQA). It includes all the areas that must be covered to attain this qualification. Students who work their way through this material, and become competent in the different areas, should be able to present themselves for formal assessment for the qualification. The full qualification is included as an appendix.

A suggested two-week course outline is also included for trainers to use in covering the material. It should be noted, though, that it would probably take more time to become fully competent in all the required areas.

These are some of the features of the toolkit:

- The learning curve: Each chapter contains a short episode in the adventures of Ace Tshabalala, an intern at Sandi FM. We hope you enjoy the story!
- Check it out! We have included a set of references for reading further. Some of these are books, others websites.
- Do it! There are also a set of exercises, to practise various skills.
- On a shoestring: Most chapters include suggestions for handling issues with little money and few resources.

I hope you enjoy this toolkit. Radio journalism is not just hard work. It's also lots of fun.

Franz Krüger

Acknowledgements

Thanks are due to many people: the students I have worked with; the staff at Jozi FM and Talk Radio 702, who allowed me to observe their hectic newsrooms; Merle Dieterich, Kieran Maree, Faiza Abrahams-Smith, Martin Vilakazi, Gilbert Mokwatedi, Mary Papayya, Kenneth Andresen, Jacob Ntshangase and Noma Rangana, for looking at the draft and giving valuable input; to Jo-Anne Richards, for editing the manuscript; to the SABC as well as Angie Kapelianis, Mercedes Besent and Solly Phetoe, who allowed the use of some of their work; to Anton Harber for the loan of a wire radio; to Mosotho Stone for technical input, compiling the recordings of audio problems and access to IAJ resources; to Noreen Alexander, for the chapter on presentation. Particular thanks are due to the IAJ and the Open Society Foundation who supported this project. As always, I am indebted to my family, Lindy, Ruth and Thomas, for ongoing love and support, and to Lindy for the drawings that go with The Learning Curve.

5FM broadcasts from a coffee shop in the foyer of the SABC's headquarters in Auckland Park

Chapter **1**

Telling news stories: Journalism and radio

The presenter slips into her seat, adjusts the microphone, and makes magic. How else can you describe it when somebody speaks to thousands, even millions, but addresses each person individually? When somebody makes pictures, using just her voice? When somebody presses the most modern digital technology into the service of that most ancient of human activities: storytelling?

Radio is a remarkable medium. In the age of the Internet, it seems old-fashioned and limited, but it remains one of the most powerful means of communication. Before we begin to consider how journalism works on radio, we need to understand some of the medium's particular characteristics.

THE LEARNING CURVE

Welcome to Sandi FM!

'Hi, I'm Liz, news editor,' said the woman with big hair from behind her computer screen. 'You must be the new intern? Amos, is it?'

'Ace, actually, Ace Tshabalala. Yes, I am,' he said, and thought, as he had so often: ace reporter.

'Well, you're welcome! Let's get some coffee, and I can fill you in.'

Off to one side there was a table with a kettle and a pile of dirty cups. As Liz turned on the kettle, she said: 'This is probably the last cup of coffee you'll get from me. So make the most of it.' Her laugh was shrill but not unfriendly.

She caught his eyes roaming the newsroom: a few terminals, phones, papers scattered over the desks. So this was Sandi FM.

'Not exactly the BBC, I know. I worked there once, you know. Bush House." She sighed.

"I'll tell you about it sometime. Here, there are just five of us full-time, but we keep those bulletins on air from six to six and then there's an hour of current affairs, too, after that. It's called newsday. Thank heavens for you interns, otherwise I don't know how we'd manage. We'll start you off on the day shift. You'll meet the others when they come in, and I'll ask one of them to show you the studios and everything else.'

She poured the coffee, and offered him a cup. 'Where do I sit?' He asked.

'Oh, you'll have to share that desk with Lerato. She's also from your technikon – what do they call it now, technical university? Lerato Moagi, do you know her? She's fabulous – I hope we can keep her when her internship's over. She's already been standing in as presenter on the current affairs show sometimes. Watch her closely, you'll learn a lot.'

But Ace had stopped listening. Lerato Moagi. Damn right she was fabulous. There was no way he could work in the same office as her, let alone share a desk.

Radio speaks to people in their own languages

The SA print media are overwhelmingly English and Afrikaans – only Zulu has significant newspapers. Television is mainly English, with the other languages squeezed together on two SABC channels. But each official language has an SABC radio station to itself, and the corporation also broadcasts in two San languages in the Northern Cape. Community stations broadcast in the languages spoken in their areas – Radio Kwezi, in Kranskop, has programmes in Zulu, English, Afrikaans, and even German, since there is a sizeable community of German farmers in the area.

Radio is cheap

A radio station can be set up relatively cheaply, which is why community radio is a viable option for poor communities. Many stations have been able to raise donor funding for studio and broadcast equipment, which is the biggest set-up expense. Running costs can be kept very low, even though survival remains a constant struggle for most community stations.

Radio is also cheap to listen to. You have to buy a newspaper every time you want to read it. TV sets are pricey, but small radio sets can be bought for as little as R20. Once you have a radio, all you pay for is the electricity it needs to run.

Radio is big

For these and other reasons, radio has the biggest audience: surveys reveal that some 90% of South Africans have access to radio. More South Africans own radios than own mattresses.[1] It is the only source of reliable information for many people, particularly in the poorer urban and rural areas, bringing them music, entertainment and news from the rest of the world. Radio is truly the people's medium.

Radio is easy and accessible

A TV news crew consists of a reporter, camera operator and sound person. A radio journalist needs no more than a tape recorder and a cellphone. At a pinch, the job can be done with nothing but eyes and ears to observe, and a voice to report.

It is very easy for the voices of ordinary people to be heard on the radio. Phone-in programmes are easy and popular, and it is also simple to get people to come into the studio to take part in a discussion. For some stations, funeral notices are an important community service: people can easily get news of a death in the family to people who may be far away.

Radio is fast

It is the fastest of all mediums. News bulletins are generally hourly, but important news doesn't even have to wait that long. With a cellphone, journalists can report live from the scene. And frequent updates mean that listeners can be kept updated on the event as it unfolds. Both TV and newspapers need several hours of production time before a report can reach the audience – although TV sometimes uses live reports, if the timing works out.

However, speed can also lead to mistakes. Pippa Green, former head of radio news at the SABC, said 'the great strength of news on radio – its swiftness – can also be its undoing. In a newspaper, there is the luxury of reading copy (in one language) usually well before deadline. ... The pressure to be first is both the tyranny and the joy of the medium.'[2]

Compare:
Circulation (2005):
   Daily Sun: 437 000 daily
   Sunday Times: 506 000 weekly
   Sowetan: 124 000 daily
   City Press: 189 000 weekly
   - Audit Bureau of Circulations
Listenership (2005):
   Ukhozi FM: 4.57m daily
   Metro FM: 2.64m daily
   East Coast: 1.2m daily
   Radio 702: 162 000 daily
   - Radio Audience Measurement Survey

Radio works with the listener's imagination

Robert McLeish writes: 'It is a blind medium which can stimulate the imagination so that as soon as a voice comes out of the loudspeaker, the listener attempts to visualise what he hears and to create in the mind's eye the owner of the voice.'[3] Feature packages, documentaries and dramas make use of these opportunities in radio. They have become rare on mainstream stations, as they take more time and money to produce. But even the quickest news story can be improved by some description that gives listeners a sense of the place and scene.

Radio relies on the human voice
Spoken language carries much more information than the written variety. It tells us about the personality and mood of the speaker: you can hear a smile in somebody's voice, the embarrassment of the government official who's been caught out, or the deep sadness of the mother whose child is missing. We place people by their accents and judge their credibility by hesitations and pauses.

Presenters (or hosts) play a crucial role in creating successful radio, and station managers choose them very carefully. More important than smooth delivery and a good command of the language is being able to project a personality that listeners like and relate to.

Radio is a part of people's lives
Radio is an intimate medium, creating the illusion that the person behind the microphone is speaking to each listener individually. It speaks to people in their cars, kitchens and bedrooms, and matches the rhythm of their lives. They wake to an early bulletin and know that if they are not driving off by the time the comedy slot begins, the kids will be late for school.

Radio fits easily into the background of listeners' lives: TV, newspapers and Internet demand undivided attention, while people more often than not listen to radio while they are driving, cooking or doing something else. The downside is that they can easily switch off – radio has to work hard to keep its audience's attention.

Radio is transient
If a listener has missed an item on the bulletin, it's gone. The radio has no rewind button. There are no second chances. A newspaper reader, by contrast, may well go over a story again if something seems unclear. Since it is also possible to misunderstand – particularly if one's attention is elsewhere – radio has to be very careful to be clear and straightforward. Icasa requires radio stations to keep an 'airtape' of everything that is broadcast so there's a record to refer to if any legal action arises.

Radio news formats

There are two main ways in which radio stations accommodate the news. They will be discussed in more detail in chapters to come, but here is a brief summary of their characteristics.

Bulletins

Most radio stations have bulletins – short news updates at the top of the hour. These can be from around two to seven, even ten minutes, in length. Peak time bulletins are often longer than those aired at other times. Individual items run to 35 to 50 seconds, depending on station style – just enough time to give the main points of a breaking news story, but not long enough to give much depth or background. Since the next bulletin is only an hour away, the format is well-suited to following the twists and turns of a developing story.

Current affairs shows

Longer news shows of an hour or more are known as current affairs shows. In South Africa, few stations outside the SABC have the resources for this format, which offers scope for a more thorough treatment of the news. A knowledgeable, personable presenter is essential for a good current affairs show, and will stitch together the different parts of the show. These may include a live interview with a minister, a packaged report on a debate in parliament, with clips from protesters outside, a short voiced report from the Middle East etc. Shows usually include regular slots, like sport and economics.

In addition to the news bulletins and current affair shows, stations use a wide range of programme formats to deal with current issues. They include:

Discussion and phone-in programmes

Talk radio has become very popular, not least because it is cheap. At its most basic, it involves somebody sitting behind the microphone and opening the lines for anybody to talk about anything at all. However, well-produced shows focus on a particular subject, invite appropriate guests and make sure that the presenter is thoroughly briefed on the issue.

These are only the most common programme types used – in fact, all kinds of other formats are used from time to time, sometimes successfully, sometimes not.

The South African radio landscape

The first three radio stations began broadcasting in South Africa in 1924. These were independent stations, licensed by the government and run by a group of amateurs in Johannesburg, the municipality in Durban and the Publicity Association in Cape Town. They quickly ran into financial trouble, and were taken over by a successful entrepreneur, I.W. Schlesinger, who linked them together to form the African Broadcasting Corporation. In 1950, the government took over broadcasting, and set up the South African Broadcasting Corporation, modelled on the BBC.[5]

Radio Bantu was introduced to serve the seven Bantu peoples of the country, according to the nature, needs and character of each, and, by encouraging language consciousness among each of the Bantu peoples, to strengthen national consciousness.
– Douglas Fuchs, SABC director-general, 1969[4]

In the early years, programming was mostly in English, although the use of Afrikaans increased, particularly after the National Party took power in 1948. As the SABC grew, it developed four different kinds of stations:

1) The English and Afrikaans services focused on 'high culture' for the two white groups.
2) African language stations, broadcast on FM.
3) Regional music-format stations, with high commercial content.
4) National commercial stations like Springbok Radio, and later Radio 5 and Metro.[7]

There were people in the news department who were telephoned daily by the Prime Minister's office. It was actually quite a circus, because you might get three or four calls about how to do the same item. ... Cabinet ministers would come in and say, 'Look, I want you to interview me tonight and here are a list of the questions you must ask me.' – Unnamed SABC TV producer[6]

'Radio Bantu' had been set up in 1960 as a separate part of the SABC, where '35 white supervisors ... controlled the output of black announcers and programmes on six channels'.[8] The SABC's roll-out of the FM transmitter network – the first exercise of its kind in the world – ensured that black audiences could get official information clearly and easily. FM-only receivers were available very cheaply, and this meant that audiences could not listen to medium wave or shortwave broadcasts from outside South Africa. Radio Bantu was designed to play a crucial role in defining apartheid-style tribal identities, closely linked to the homeland system.

Apartheid ideology, however, also created a gap for a new kind of radio station. The Pretoria government wanted to create 'independent' homelands, and needed to give them various things to make 'independence' seem real, including their own radio stations. This allowed Capital Radio to begin operating from the Wild Coast in 1979, under the supposed authority of the Transkei government, and Radio 702 similarly from Bophutatswana. Both were commercial stations, and developed a reputation for independent news coverage.

As the process of democratisation got underway with the release of Nelson Mandela in 1990, the reform of broadcasting was seen as urgent. A number of steps were taken:

• The Independent Broadcasting Authority (IBA) was set up to license radio and television stations. It later merged with the SA Telecommunications Regulatory Authority (Satra) to form Icasa, the Independent Communications Authority of SA.
• The signal distribution functions of the SABC were split off into a separate organisation, Sentech.
• A new board was appointed for the SABC in an open and democratic way.
• New SABC management tried to bring it into line with the new South Africa's democratic values.

- The SABC's regional commercial stations were sold off to private business.
- The SABC's 11 language stations were upgraded, renamed and given mandates to focus more on their listeners.
- The IBA licensed several new commercial radio stations in different urban areas, including Kaya FM, YFM and P4 Radio. A new private TV station, e.tv, was also licensed.
- Community radio licences were issued, leading to dramatic growth in this sector.

Licences and formats

The new broadcasting dispensation provided for three kinds of radio licence:

- Public broadcasting – essentially the SABC's services
- Commercial broadcasting – stations operating for profit
- Community broadcasting – known in other parts of the world as local radio.

Radio stations can also be described in terms of their programming. In other countries, radio stations have become very tightly 'niched' – they are designed to appeal to a very small section of the population. In many American cities, you can tune in to an astounding range of radio stations: one playing only country and western music, another playing classical, another rock, yet another concentrating on news, even weather. In South Africa, the trend towards niche broadcasting is visible, but less developed. Few stations, here and elsewhere, fall neatly into the following categories – they are mixed.

Full-spectrum

The SABC's language stations try to appeal to all listeners who use a particular language. They will include everything from children's programmes to funeral notices, play many different kinds of music and include information for poor and rich, urban and rural, unemployed, student and churchgoer. They tend to have a strong public service mandate.

Music stations

Many South African commercial stations play mostly music, and choose the style of music that is appealing to their chosen audience. There are 'adult contemporary' stations, 'contemporary hit radio' and others. The more successful stations of this kind are very strict about the music they play. They give their DJs a rigid playlist, from which they are not allowed to depart.

Talk

Talk Radio 702 pioneered the talk format in South Africa: strong on news, the programming relies heavily on discussion programmes and listener participation through phone-ins. More recently, SAfm has turned more and more to talk, although it still has some features of full-spectrum broadcasting, like church services and music slots.

I first experienced the value of community radio in the ALX FM studios just after it had begun broadcasting in 1996. It was 1 o'clock in the afternoon, just after the news. Suddenly the door to the studio was flung open and a distraught woman rushed in. 'My little boy! I lost him at the corner of Selborne Street and 6th Avenue. He's wearing a blue jersey and a green cap. Please help me find him!' The presenter immediately interrupted the music and broadcast the emergency message. Less than ten minutes later a lady from a spaza shop brought him in. She had been listening to ALX FM and her shop was on Selborne. She looked out of her door and saw the little boy at once and quickly brought him to the station. That reminded me of the 'extended family' of a community radio station. People become related through listening to the station, as if they were responding to the sound of a drum beating out messages. – John van Zyl[10]

Community

The Jabulani! Freedom of the Airwaves conference in Holland in 1991 had called for a community radio sector that would be 'participatory, ... owned and controlled by the community itself, and the broadcasting content of the station should be determined by the needs of community as perceived by that community'.[9]

The new broadcasting dispensation made room for this kind of station, and some 120 now operate around the country. They tend to serve poorer communities with a mixture of music and talk, often having to rely on volunteers and very few resources. Despite many obstacles, they have done much to enrich both their communities and the broadcasting landscape.

Regulation

Around the world, radio stations are licensed because the frequency spectrum is a limited resource. In South Africa, Icasa issues licences after a detailed inquiry, and on the basis of a frequency plan that determines which frequencies are available for different station categories in a particular area.

Licences come with conditions which set out the proportion of talk and music the station has to use, the strength of the signal, the languages and many other things. Icasa's Broadcasting Monitoring and Complaints Commission (BMCC) makes sure these conditions are not broken.

Stations must also stick to a Code of Conduct (see Appendix 1), which covers things like the depiction of violence and sex, the use of bad language and other issues. However, stations that are members of the National Association of Broadcasters – the public and commercial stations, as well as a few community stations – fall under a different body, the Broadcasting Complaints Commission of SA (BCCSA). Members of the public who have complaints about a broadcast – including a news item – can complain to the BCCSA, which can impose a fine of up to R40 000 if it finds against the station.

The state of radio news

The SABC remains the organisation that devotes most resources to radio news. According to former head of radio news Pippa Green, it has ten newsrooms around the country. They work in 13 languages (the 11 official languages plus two San languages) and produce 36 hours of current affairs and many bulletins a day.[11] SABC stations are virtually the only ones whose shows include produced packages which exploit the great potential for sound. However, the size of the organisation and a bureaucratic culture sometimes make the news slow and ponderous.

News is expensive, and many commercial stations try to meet their licence requirements for regular newscasts as cheaply as possible. This means their news tends to consist only of brief, fast-paced bulletins. People working in these environments get very skilled at re-angling and re-working stories, to keep them sounding fresh through successive bulletins. The stations rely heavily on getting sound from telephone interviews or from secondary sources like TV, and their reporters in some cases rarely move out of the office.

Stations like Talk Radio 702 and its younger sister 567 Cape Talk are exceptions to this pattern. Although they don't make much use of lengthy produced pieces, they are very strong on the live reporting of breaking stories, often from the scene. They also often manage to pack a lot of sound into a short bulletin item.

CHECK IT OUT!

- Radio: Theatre of the mind, in: AS De Beer (ed): Mass media towards the millennium.
- Robert McLeish: Radio Production, Ch 1
- Icasa website: www.icasa.org.za
- Broadcasting Complaints Commission of SA website: www.bccsa.co.za
- National Community Radio Forum website: www.ncrf.org.za
- SABC website: www.sabc.co.za
- World Association of Community Broadcasters website: www.amarc.org
- ABC Ulwazi website: www.abculwazi.org.za

Community stations invariably regard news as an important element of their programming, and set out to concentrate on local news. But a lack of resources and skills make it hard to do this well. Too often, they end up reading items out of a local newspaper, sometimes without even crediting the paper. Line-ups usually include current affairs, but this often consists simply of long discussions, not always well prepared.

Newsroom organisation and roles

There are many different ways in which newsrooms are organised. In small organisations, a couple of people do almost everything. In large organisations, there are many specialists. In some instances, people rotate through different roles. The following are the basic functions found in most radio newsrooms.

News editor
S/he holds the newsroom together, assigning, briefing and debriefing reporters. A good news editor will keep a diary, a daily list of stories being worked on, to make sure that no important stories are missed, and to keep track of what everybody is doing. S/he also edits scripts of news reports before the reporter records them. The news editor is usually a member of the station's management team, reporting to the station manager.

Reporters
Reporters gather the news. They attend media conferences, interview people, always hunting for a new story and angle. They write and produce the reports that are used in the bulletins and current affairs shows. Reporters need a lively curiosity, they should be prepared to work fast and hard and care deeply about getting the details right.

Larger organisations may have specialist reporters for areas like sport, business, health and others.

Newsreaders
There used to be a strict division between those who report and those who read the news bulletins. It was felt that newsreaders needed a 'golden voice'. They were often actors rather than journalists. That distinction has mostly disappeared, but it remains important for a newsreader to have good presentation skills.

Bulletin producers or compilers
On many stations, the newsreader also compiles the bulletin. Sometimes, this function is given to a separate person. It involves choosing stories, writing them appropriately for the audience and allotted time, and deciding in which order to run them.

Presenters (hosts or anchors)

The person who hosts an entire show is the presenter. S/he gives the programme its personality, holds it together and makes sure that it flows well. Good presenters are very valuable, and can command good salaries.

Producers

Presenters usually rely very heavily on their producer – the person behind the scenes who keeps the show on track. This means lining up interviewees, deciding on a running order or when an interview needs to end. Some shows have large teams of producers.

Controllers (technical producers or engineers)

In many stations, the DJ or presenter has to operate the mixing desk while on air – this is known as a 'self-op' studio. In others, a controller looks after the sound of the show. This means putting callers on air and playing ad spots, music or other features at the right time, as directed by the producer. Above all, it means making sure that the technical quality of the broadcast is of the highest standard.

DO IT!

1) By watching and interviewing them, find out how four different friends or family members use radio, and write a page on your observation of each one.
   a. When do they listen?
   b. What do they listen to?
   c. What are they doing while they listen?
   d. What makes them choose particular stations and programmes?
   e. How much do they remember of particular programmes or news bulletins?
   Discuss your findings.
2) Listen to half an hour of PM Live (SAfm). Keeping a close eye on your watch, write down how the programme develops. For each item, you should indicate what the item is about, how long it is and what kind of contribution it is. Keep an ear open for any regular slots, like finance, weather or sport.
3) Listen to news programmes on three different stations: SAfm, a community station and a commercial station in your area. Listen also to World Radio Network, which is on air on SAfm after midnight and relays the programmes of a selection of broadcasters from other countries.
   a. Who is the audience?
   b. What formats do they use for news?
   c. How long are the bulletins, and any other news shows?
   d. What kinds of contributions do they use for the news?
   e. If they have a news show, how is it structured?
   f. Does their approach to news fit the audience? How?
   g. What kind of resources do you think they need to produce news?
   Discuss your findings.
4) Visit a station in your area, and spend time with people in the newsroom. Watch how they work, and talk to them about how they do news. But don't get in the way!

Stringers (correspondents)

Many stations rely on stringers to tip off the newsroom about events that need covering, or even to file stories on them. The difference between them and reporters is that they are not employed at the station. They may live in an outlying area, and stay in touch with the newsroom by phone.

1 Rod Amner, *Getting Radio Active. Leading Edge*, Vol 7. Cape Town: Independent Development Trust, 1996, quoted in AS de Beer. (1998). *Mass Media Towards the Millennium: The South Afrcan Handbook of Mass Communication*. Pretoria: JL van Schaik Publishers, p151
2 Pippa Green, *Reporting for Radio*. In: Adrian Hadland (ed), *Changing the Fourth Estate: Essays on South African Journalism*. Cape Town: HSRC Press, 2005. p194.
3 Rober McLeish, Radio Production. Oxford: Focal Press. P1
4 Quoted in Keyan Tomaselli & Ruth Tomaselli, *Between Policy and Practice in the SABC, 1970 - 1981*, in: Ruth Tomaselli, Keyan Tomaselli & Johan Muller (eds), *Currents of Power: State Broadcasting in South Africa*. Bellville: Anthropos, 1989. 95
5 Graham Hayman & Ruth Tomaselli, *Ideology and Technology in the Growth of South African Broadcasting 1924 - 1971*. In Ruth Tomaselli, Keyan Tomaselli & Johan Muller (Eds) *Currents of Power: State Broadcasting in South Africa*. Bellville: Anthropos, 1989.
6 quoted in ibid, 95
7 Ruth Teer-Tomaselli & Coenie De Villiers, *Radio: Theatre of the Mind*. In AS De Beer (Ed), *Mass Media Towards the Millennium: The South African Handbook of Mass Communication*. Pretoria: J.L. van Schaik, 1998. p 156
8 Ibid
9 Quoted in John Van Zyl, *A Sense of Belonging: Community Radio and Civil Society*. Braamfontein: ABC Ulwazi, 2005. 9
10 Van Zyl: John van Zyl, *A Sense of Belonging: Community Radio and Civil Society*. Braamfontein: ABC Ulwazi, 2005. 7
11 Pippa Green, op cit, p 195

A politician besieged by journalists after an election

Chapter **2**

A deep mystery: What makes news?

Ask editors on any newspaper, TV or radio station what they look for in a journalist, and high on their wish list will be a 'good news sense'. Journalists find it hard to explain exactly what guides them, and so they rely on a kind of instinct – it's a strong story because it feels like a strong story.

Others – from media studies academics to beginner journalists struggling to please a tough news editor – have tried to work out what turns one bit of information into news, but not another. Some of the elements that make something 'newsworthy' include:

THE LEARNING CURVE

A Dead Horse

'Gather around, let's talk diaries,' Liz called. The three journalists turned vaguely in her direction: Jack, Thatho and Lerato. Lerato was wearing tight jeans and a white t-shirt, her hair intricately braided. Ace sighed and pulled his chair closer. 'What have we got?' Liz asked.

Lerato spoke up. 'I wanted to look at this issue of sanitation. There are all those squatter areas with no toilets – it's a huge health problem.'

'And so what? You keep going on about this kind of stuff. How often do I have to tell you: a problem's not a story – give me something new,' said Liz. 'You're just flogging a dead horse. No, I think you need to go to court. That rapist is appearing, the one that raped those three little girls. There's likely to be a demonstration – take a minidisk.'

Ace saw Lerato's nostrils flare as she bent down to make a note. The meeting went on: more court cases, a media conference by the municipality about a housing project, calls to the police, somebody had phoned about a missing relative, a taxi accident. At the end, Liz turned to Ace: 'Just check with the community helpline people whether there's anything worth doing. Lerato will show you.'

On the way to the office where Sandi FM offered paralegal assistance to the community, Ace said to Lerato: 'I thought that idea about sanitation was a good one. It's a big issue.'

'Well, you're not the news editor, are you?' she snapped, and turned on her heel to head back to the newsroom.

New

The word news itself points to the first element: it needs to be new. Something has just happened, or it's just been found out. When archaeologists found a fossilised human footprint on the West Coast of South Africa, the footprint itself was obviously not new. But its discovery was. And a story about corruption at a parastatal is a big story, even if it happened some time ago.

Important

Things that have a direct impact on people's lives make news. Tax increases, a strike by municipal workers, crime statistics and much else fall into this category.

About power

People with power make news, and the more powerful they are, the more likely it is that they will get covered. If the local principal opens a science lab, only the school newspaper will be interested. If it's the provincial MEC, the regional media will attend. If it's the president, the national media will pay attention. Even though power makes news, it is important to distinguish between things that are really important or interesting, and those that are not. Even the president sometimes makes speeches that are of little consequence.

'Steven McBride is 20 years old.'
So what? It might be information, but it's not news.

'Half his short life has been spent in prisons, borstals (reform schools) and other institutions.'

Well, that's sad and may be of some interest to somebody because it is unusual, but it is still not news.

'Steven McBride is coming out today ... a free man.'

It is information, it has some interest and it is new because he is coming out today, but it is still not news.

'Three months ago, McBride was sentenced to life for the murder of his parents.'

His parents. Now this is important. How can a man who has been charged with murdering his parents be let out of prison after only three months?

'New evidence has come to light to show conclusively that McBride did not commit the murders and that the killer is still on the loose and has already struck again.'

The information is new, interesting, and important, but for it to be newsworthy, it would have to be relevant to you, the audience. If the murders were committed in your home town – that is news – and local radio and TV would almost certainly run it as their lead. - Andrew Boyd[1]

Confirm beliefs

It may seem to contradict the previous point, but some stories are selected because they confirm people's prejudices. We expect conflict from the Middle East, and so stories about mayhem there run easily. Stories that contain heroes and villains fit easily into people's moral worldview – journalism is not very good at portraying complex individuals who have good and bad in them.

Interesting

People are generally interested in what's happening around them: the lives of the rich and famous, natural disasters, a new shopping centre in town. Anything that people are likely to talk about will make a good news story.

Dramatic and surprising

News needs to make people sit up and say: 'wow, that's amazing! I didn't know that.' Car chases, sieges, cash-in-transit robberies and mountain rescues are full of drama, and make interesting news.

About personalities

People who are already famous get news coverage very easily. Pop star Brenda Fassie captured the public imagination, and anything she did made news. Even after her death, people connected to her get media attention just because of the association. And newspapers know that they will sell extra copies if they can find a reason to have Nelson Mandela on the front page.

Big

The bigger an event, the more likely it is to get coverage. Rightly or wrongly, a taxi accident in which one person dies will get less attention than one in which 17 people die.

Near

Human beings are much more interested in things that happen nearby, or to people they can identify with. Residents of Witbank would be fascinated by a fire in a shopping centre there – people in Cape Town would not pay much attention to it. 'Huge problems for them are less important than small problems for us,' writes Andrew Boyd.[2]

25

Conflict

People are always interested in fights – the more dramatic the better. Wars, messy divorces, strikes and land invasions are all different kinds of conflicts. This value is also a reason for the enduring interest in sport, where teams and players 'fight' for glory.

Human

Stories about people we can identify with attract our attention. A disabled athlete from a poor community who does well will become a darling of the media because listeners admire his courage and achievement. A story about a kidnapped child also draws audiences: they identify with the anguish of the parents, and share their desperate hope for the child to be found.

Available

Stories only become news if journalists can find out about them. This means that things happening in towns and cities are more likely to get covered than those in the countryside, since they are easier to get to. People with telephones are more likely to be asked for their opinions than those without. Similarly, stories will fall through the cracks if they happen at the wrong time. A Namibian newspaper missed the suicide of a prominent corruption suspect because it happened after their deadline.

Includes strong audio

Newspapers sometimes use a story just because it includes a good photograph, and television does the same when there is good footage. Similarly, a radio story may be chosen over another just because there is a strong soundbite available. Or a radio feature may get used because of the way the reporter has used ambient sound.

'Fits in'

Newspapers have pages for particular subjects, like world news, and some stories will be chosen simply because the sub-editors need an international story. In radio, too, some stories may be chosen simply for 'balance', or because the station insists that a bulletin must end with a light, funny story.

Decisions, decisions ...

Every day, a vast number of events and stories fight for attention. The news agencies are always busy, churning out thousands of words every

Seek out 'fires, explosions, floods ... railway accidents, destructive storms, earth-quakes, shipwrecks ... accidents ... street riots ... strikes .. the suicide of persons of note, social or political and murders of a sensational or atrocious character.' – Reuters instruction to journalists, 1880[3]

'News is something someone, somewhere doesn't want you to print. The rest is advertising.' – Anon[4]

'News is the first rough draft of history.' – Ben Bradlee[5]

'Journalism largely consists of saying 'Lord Jones is dead' to people who never knew Lord Jones was alive.' – GK Chesterton[6]

'Yesterday's newspaper is used to wrap fish and yesterday's broadcast does not exist at all.' – Martin Mayer[7]

People might think they want good news and say they want good news, but what they actually read is bad news. Bad news is vivid; good news usually means complicated committee resolutions and proceedings. It's not that editors are ghouls; it's that people are more gripped by a snake striking than a doe grazing. – Denis Beckett[8]

day. Things are happening, even in the quietest community: court cases, traffic accidents, disputes, local organisations are having meetings, crime, new projects begin etc etc. Newsrooms – and individual journalists – have to make choices. They have to decide which stories to follow and which to leave.

Working journalists use the news values listed above to make those decisions, even if they do so by feel and instinct, rather than consciously. Those decisions are also a matter of individual judgment. If you give a number of editors the same set of stories to look at, the chances are their decisions will be similar in some respects – but there will also be differences.

News is a construction; it is made. Something only becomes news once it is actually on air or in print. One can answer the question at the head of this chapter briefly and perhaps a little cynically by saying: news is news because the media say it is.

What influences the decisions journalists make?

Audience
Many of the news values outlined have to be considered in relation to a particular audience. Obviously, they are not all the same. A station like Classic FM appeals to business people; Yfm is targeted at the youth, a community station like Radio Kwezi is talking to the community in the Kranskop area. And so their news bulletins will be quite different.

Before a new radio station is started, research is done to gain an understanding of the target audience. This helps in giving them the music and information they want. It can be expensive and sophisticated, or quite simple. People involved in community radio sometimes go door-to-door to find out more about their community.

Journalists need a good understanding of who they are talking to. The Daily Sun newspaper has a big figure of a man in a blue overall in its entrance hall, to remind everybody working there who the audience is.

Commercial interest
Commercial radio stations choose an audience on the basis that they will be able to sell advertising to companies who are interested in this market. But public and community broadcasters are also interested in advertising to cover their costs, even if they are not broadcasting in order to make money. Choices about programming are made in order to attract the target audience – and this translates into advertising revenue. There is nothing wrong with this, as long as the news remains complete, reliable and credible. It becomes a problem if

commercial interests dictate news content directly. This would be the case if, for instance, a story about rotten chicken being sold in a local supermarket was suppressed because the station wanted advertising from that shop.

Bias and 'objectivity'

Everybody has their own values and interests, and it would be unrealistic to expect journalists to leave these behind when they are doing their work. But at the same time, biased reporting is not credible.

Until around World War II, newspapers were unashamedly full of propaganda. But then, writes Stuart Allan, technological and other changes in the newspaper industry led to the development of a new ideal: objectivity.[9] Journalists wanted to be seen as professionals, as impartial observers of events. In the last few years, the idea has fallen from favour again, because its limitations have been recognised.

But fairness remains an important element of journalistic ethics. We may not be able to stand completely aloof from the world and our own backgrounds and beliefs, but we can make sure we give both sides of the story. And we can make sure of our facts.

So, is community radio different?

Mainstream news values have come in for a lot of criticism, but in fact there are more similarities between community radio journalism and everyone else than people sometimes admit. John van Zyl, of ABC Ulwazi, writes: 'Traditional news values do apply, but there are also specific issues that make community radio different. Community radio news is unique as it:

• Reflects the concerns of the community and various members.
• Highlights news happenings in your area – whether these are tragic or joyous.
• Acts as a barometer for listeners to measure how important issues (such as the Budget speech or petrol increases) will affect them.'[10]

At bottom, community radio should be in tune with the people it broadcasts to – which is not so very different from a commercial radio station focusing on its audience. In addition, of course, its purpose is not to make money, but to serve the community, and this will shape the choices it makes in news and other areas.

But similar kinds of news will interest all audiences: stories about people, stories that affect and interest listeners and so on.

CHECK IT OUT!
• Andrew Boyd, Broadcast journalism. Oxford: Focal Press, 2002. Ch 2.
• Stuart Allan, News culture. Buckingham: Open University Press, 1999. Ch 3.
• Fairness & accuracy in reporting (Fair) critiques the way mainstream US media cover the news. Check out their website, www.fair.org.
• The Media Monitoring Project monitors the media in SA. Check out their website at www.mediamonitoring.org.za

DO IT!

1) Listen to a bulletin on your favourite station, making detailed notes about the stories you hear. Then for each story, list the news values which earned it a place in the bulletin.

2) You are compiling the 1pm bulletin for Umhlobo Wenene, based in Port Elizabeth. It is heard in seven out of South Africa's nine provinces, but its core listenership area is the Eastern Cape. You have the following stories to choose from, but you can choose only five stories. Which ones do you use? Indicate the order in which you would place them in the bulletin. Motivate your decisions.

a) US president George W Bush announces that US bombers have hit targets in Iran overnight. He says they destroyed chemical weapons that were about to be launched at Israel. But he says this is not yet the beginning of war.

b) A truck overturned on the N2 highway near Port Elizabeth, spilling tons of mealies onto the road. People from the township took the mealies, but 15 have got very sick because the food was bad.

c) The mayor of Umtata has opened a new community centre in the city. In his speech, he said the city council was determined to help the people and would fight poverty every way they could.

d) President Thabo Mbeki has chaired a meeting of African heads of state in Addis Ababa, where he called on them to ratify the establishment of a security organ for the continent.

e) Finance Minister Trevor Manuel has announced that tax will be reduced in the new budget. Some economists are quoted as saying this might include zero-rating of basic foods (no VAT on bread, mealies, milk etc).

f) The strike at Delta Motor Corporation in Port Elizabeth has entered its second week, with talks between union and management deadlocked. The workers want a 13% increase, the company says it can only afford 7%. Another meeting is due to be held later today.

g) The Eastern Cape provincial government in Bisho has appealed for people to plant trees, to make the townships look prettier.

h) A Soweto principal has been arrested for raping three teenage girls at his school.

i) Terrible floods in Limpopo province have left thousands homeless. Provincial authorities have declared an emergency, and the death toll is said to be 27.

1 Andrew Boyd, *Broadcast Journalism*. Oxford: Focal Press, 2002. p 23
2 Ibid. p 19
3 Quoted in Gwen Ansell, *Basic Journalism*. Milpark: M&G books, 2002. p 1
4 Boyd, op cit, p 28
5 Quoted in *A Writer's Resource*, on the website of the Illinois Wesleyan University. Accessed at http://titan.iwu.edu/~jplath/Quoth.html#Journalists on 15 March 2006.
6 Boyd, op cit, p 20
7 Boyd, op cit, p 20
8 *Newshound Denis Beckett on News*, in Francois Nel, Writing for the media in Southern Africa. Cape Town: Oxford University Press, 2005. p 66
9 Stuart Allan, *News Culture*. Buckingham: Open University Press, 2001. pp 12-26
10 John Van Zyl, *Community Radio: the People's Voice*, Johannesburg: Sharp Sharp Media, 2003. p 58

Trainees on a course practice their interviewing skills

Chapter 3

The heart of the hunter: Reporting

The idea

When journalists first arrive in the newsroom, as interns, trainees or volunteers, they are mostly told what stories to work on. If they are lucky, they will get briefed properly. If they are not, they run the risk of getting the story badly wrong. Preparation is everything, even for the simplest story. It's the news editor's responsibility to brief reporters properly, to make sure that they have enough

THE LEARNING CURVE

Breaking Story

Liz put down the phone and called: 'Somebody's just phoned to say three kids from Luanda, that squatter area on the airport road, have been taken to hospital, very sick. Apparently they were playing in dirty water, and residents are blaming the municipality for not putting in proper toilets. Thatho: we need some kind of confirmation from the hospital. Lerato: can you get out there and see whether you can find the families. We'll take it from there.'

The newsroom sprang into action. Lerato grabbed a minidisk and dashed out with a toss of her head and a grin on her face. Thatho called the hospital superintendent, who confirmed that three children of 4, 5 and 8 had been admitted to hospital with typhoid. They were in a serious condition. She recorded him directly into the PC, and cut a clip that would be available for the next bulletin.

'We need the municipality, now, Thatho. Can you get onto that?' said Liz. 'Typhoid. Isn't that the disease that wiped out half of Europe in the Middle Ages?' Her eye fell on Ace. 'Can you use the Internet?'

'Of course,' he said, drawing himself up.

'See what you can find out about it. Particularly whether there's a connection to poor sanitation. While you're there, see whether you can find an expert for us.'

Ace pulled his chair over to a PC and logged on. A quick look at Wikipedia, the free shared encyclopedia (www.wikipedia.com) showed that typhoid was most often spread through contact with human faeces. A google search found a summary of international campaigns for better sanitation, which also mentioned typhoid. And a quick search on the website of the local university found the phone number for the department of communicable diseases.

Ace briefed Liz on what he'd found. 'There was a woman called Typhoid Mary in New York in the early years of the last century. She was a cook who infected hundreds of people, and wouldn't stop until they dragged her off to quarantine,' he finished.

'Well done,' she said. 'Can you write a few pars of briefing notes for the presenter of Newsday this evening. And see whether you can set up one of the university people for an interview tonight. We want to know what it is, and particularly what people should do if they are not sure whether the water is safe.'

Ace picked up the phone. It was turning out to be a good day

information to do a good job. That includes background on the story, as well as a clear indication of what kind of story the desk expects. You'll approach a story very differently if you're just doing a voicer for the lunchtime news, or if you're expected to do a package for the evening current affairs show. All journalists, including interns, should insist on being briefed properly, even if time it tight.

As journalists get more experienced, the newsdesk expects them to come up with their own ideas. And there's nothing that will impress the news editor more than an intern or trainee coming up with his or her own workable ideas.

Where do ideas come from?

Seven habits of highly successful journalists:

1) Follow up
The easiest way to find ideas for stories is by taking a story that has been reported on, and asking: what happens next? A teacher is arrested for raping a pupil. The obvious follow-up is reporting the court case. But there are others: what happens to the rape survivor? How are her marks affected? If he is ultimately found guilty, there might be a story about what happens to his post at the school. (Stories of this kind must be handled very sensitively, and this will be discussed in more detail in Ch 13.)

2) Keep your eyes and ears open
Stuff is always happening. Great stories often start with an observant journalist noticing that there's a new building going up, that a shop was open for just one month and then went out of business or that a line of trucks rumbled through town at 2am. It's also important to pay attention to what people are talking about. Somebody at a party might be talking about how they reported a stolen cellphone, and the charge office had been refurbished. Hey presto: a story about improvements to the police station might be interesting to a community radio station.

3) Ask questions
Wonder about things. Wondering about the shop that was open for just a month might lead to a story about bankruptcies or – who knows – some scam or other. If you have a question about something, chances are your listeners might have the same question.

4) Think laterally
It's important to let your mind play. Seeing somebody talking on a cellphone while driving may suggest a story about the way the police are approaching minor offences, or telephone etiquette, or road safety campaigns, or developments in wireless technologies.

5) Watch other media
Pack journalism is when journalists all follow the same story like a flock of sheep. There are some major stories that nobody can really ignore, but there are also many ways in which other radio stations, TV and newspapers can help us generate original ideas. They may be missing an angle or a story, and even an advert may suggest an idea. A story about disaster relief after a hurricane in the US may suggest one about local emergency services.

6) Build contacts, and stay in touch with them

A journalist's most valuable asset is a contact book. It's important to get to know people who may have information that is newsworthy. If you're on the political beat, you need the phone numbers of relevant political leaders. The better you know what is happening in their world, the more likely it is that you will know when a story is brewing. They may also tip you off about stories.

Most newsrooms have a daily routine to call police, fire brigade, traffic police emergency services and others, just to check on any important incidents.

In this day and age, developing a beat also involves keeping an eye on the relevant websites and online communities. You may need to join a listserv, or regularly visit particular discussion forums.

7) Ideas are valuable. Collect them

Keep notes on ideas you have, as well as newspaper clippings and other items that you may use as the basis of a story. On a dry day, you can look through old ideas.

A story idea needs to be:

Interesting

Stories need to make people sit up and say: well, that's interesting. They need to pass the 'so what' test.

Appropriate for the audience

If you're working for Classic FM, whose audience consists mostly of white men over the age of 40, a story about a kwaito star might not go very far.

Doable

You need to be realistic about what can be done, in terms of the time and cost involved and the availability of sources. Many commercial radio stations run a very tight ship, and their journalists hardly move out of the office. A station like that is very unlikely to release you for three days to do a radio feature on land reform.

DO IT!

1) Have a look at any newspaper, and develop some ideas. You should find:
   a. Three follow-ups, and
   b. Three other story ideas.
   In each case, you should indicate the angle, motivate why it would be interesting, identify the sources you will need to speak to and any logistical considerations.
2) Write a short paragraph outlining an entirely original story idea that you would like to pursue.

Possible sources:
- Eyewitnesses
- People affected
- Experts
- Spokespeople
- Whistleblowers
- Documents
- Information on the Internet
- Newspaper clippings
- Phone books
- NGOs & other organisations
- And many others

Pitches and angles

Francois Nel[1] points out that there's a difference between a topic and a story. 'A topic becomes a story idea when it is clearly defined – it has a news peg, an angle, and appropriate sources,' he writes. 'House prices is a topic. The release of a new report could be a news peg. The angle could be what that means for first-time buyers.'

Journalists need to 'pitch' their idea to the newseditor, who has to be persuaded that it will be worth the time and effort. To do this properly, you need to be clear what makes it worth doing. It is important to be very clear on the angle. It's no good waffling vaguely about house prices, to stay with Nel's example. Be quick, to the point and assertive. News editors are busy people.

Getting the information

In radio, the next deadline is less than an hour away. So don't waste time. For a bulletin piece, it's often a question of phoning one or two people, getting the details and some sound, then writing the copy and editing a clip.

You can save a lot of time by going to the right person from the start. A good contact book is crucial and you need to know who, in an organisation, is allowed to and likely to speak. Police spokespeople, for instance, have a duty roster: if you phone the spokesperson who's just come off duty and poured himself a stiff drink after long hours of fielding calls, you'll waste precious time and irritate him as well.

Don't be brushed off. If a personal assistant says the person you need is in a meeting and offers to take a message, leave one but don't rely on it. Rather phone back. Otherwise your message may well go onto a pile of other messages, and you may wait forever.

Try to get estimates of when your source will become available, or information on where they are so you can track them down. Cellphone numbers are invaluable, and well worth collecting. Remember that you're the one who's in a hurry.

Always look for backup options. If the best person is uncontactable, try for somebody else. That may mean changing the angle on the story, and coming back to the original one later. For instance, if you can't get comment from the company spokesperson on the ongoing strike, perhaps you can get union comment and come back to the company for a later bulletin.

Many radio newsrooms rely almost entirely on this kind of quick-fix reporting. Reporters rarely go out of the office, and the bulletins consist almost entirely of phone clips from official spokespeople. This is often dictated by very tight budgets, but it does make for a very limited kind of news.

Planning your newsgathering

If there is space for more ambitious reporting, you need to think a little more about where and how to get the information you need. Always aim to get more information than you are going to put in the story. It allows you to choose the best material, and it ensures that you have enough contextual understanding to report clearly and accurately. As with so many other things, it's good to have a plan. The more complex the reporting task , the more you will need to plan. But even relatively simple stories benefit from asking yourself:

What information do I need?
If your story has a clear focus, you should also be able to determine what kind of information you need. What do you know? What do you need to know?

Who has this information?
Obviously, there's little point in asking the leader of an opposition party what the government is planning to do about crime. All she will be able to give you is her party's opinion.

What kind of audio material do I need?
Depending on the story, station policy and other factors, you will need to consider whether you can live with phone-quality sound, or if you need sound from a face-to-face interview. You may also need ambient sound. All these things will affect your plan. If you're just looking for a 20-second clip for the bulletin, it's a waste to schedule a one-hour in-depth interview.

How much time do I have / do I need?
The more complex or ambitious the story is, the more time it will probably need. That means that if time is tight, it may be necessary to scale back the idea, negotiate for more time, or put it off to an easier day.

Sources: handle with care

Former *Sunday Times* investigative reporter Mzilikazi wa Afrika writes: 'For any journalist, a reliable source of information is a treasure to cherish and guard with his or her life.'[2] But how can we tell whether a source is reliable?

DO IT!
1) Listen carefully to a bulletin, and identify the sources quoted in three stories. Can you think of other sources that could have been used?
2) Ask colleagues whether you can have a look at their contact books, and compare them.
3) If you haven't already done so, start your own contact book.

News sites:
Independent Newspapers:
www.iol.co.za
Media24: www.news24.com
Mail&Guardian: www.mg.co.za
Sunday Times:
www.sundaytimes.co.za
SABC: www.sabcnews.com
Business Day: www.businessday.co.za
BBC: news.bbc.co.uk
Allafrica: www.allafrica.com
Talk Radio 702: www.702.co.za
CNN: www.cnn.com
Other links on www.journalism.co.za

For one thing, there's the source's track record. Has their information proved reliable in the past?

We should also ask ourselves whether the source is in a position to know whatever it is they are telling us. Somebody may offer us details of an argument at an ANC national executive committee meeting. But if it turns out they weren't there, it would be best to treat the information with some suspicion. It seems like an obvious point, but it's amazing how many journalists fail to check.

Many sources give us information in the hope of furthering some agenda. They may hope to influence an internal party dispute by feeding out information that's unflattering to the other side, or they may hope to harm their employer by tipping us off about corrupt practices. The information may still be accurate, and worth using, but it's important to factor in the motive.

Information that is controversial must be corroborated. The more serious the claims are, the more care must be taken to find additional evidence.

The relationship between source and journalist is a complex one, and raises many ethical issues. It will be discussed further in chapter 13.

Computer-aided journalism

The Internet has made unimaginably vast amounts of information available to journalists on their desktops. With a few clicks of the mouse button, you can access details about a music star's biography, read the text of a government report or listen in on a highly technical discussion about pathologists' take on poisoning as a murder method. No journalist can afford to neglect learning the skills necessary to use this amazing resource. It's an ongoing project, as new technologies are developing all the time.

Here are some of the resources available on the Internet:

Google and other search engines
When people think about using the Internet, they generally think of Google, which is the best and most popular search engine. It has many useful features, allowing searches for images, scholarly work and others. When you know an organisation's name, but not their web address, the 'I'm feeling lucky' option often takes you straight to the site you need. It's worth spending a bit of time exploring the advanced page, which allows you to search through a particular website, among other features. A relatively new feature is the 'news alert': if you have a particular interest in the cashew nut industry, for instance, you can ask it to send you daily listings of anything published anywhere on cashews.

Although Google is the best, it's worth remembering that there are other search engines as well. Have a look at Ask Jeeves (www.ask.com), for instance, which lets you type in whole questions.

Newspaper archives

A quick way to find background information on a running story is to look at the archive of one of the websites run by major news organisations. They all have internal search functions that allow you to search for articles on a particular subject. But remember that they may contain mistakes.

Reference

A whole set of reference works is posted online, from dictionaries to atlases and compilations of quotes. Check out the 'tools' button on www.journalism. co.za for a selection. Say there's a coup attempt in Togo: you can find useful background information on the country in the CIA's factbook (www.cia.gov/cia/ publications/factbook/). The BBC (address in box) also maintains a very useful profile on all countries.

Original documents

The South African government posts many documents on its main website, www.gov.za. You can read up the text of a bill before parliament, or reports it has commissioned, or search back through an archive of media releases and speeches. Various NGOs also post documents of relevance to them.

Online databases

In the US, many databases are available online. In South Africa, there are not many, although this will undoubtedly grow. Company registration details are already available online.

Email

This allows you to get in direct touch with somebody, even if a personal assistant is blocking phone calls. Of course, it won't give you sound, but it may give you information you need, or allow you to plead directly for an interview. Newspapers have sometimes conducted entire interviews by email.

DO IT!

1) Find ten sites that deal with subjects you report on from time to time, and add them to your list of favourites.
2) Join a relevant listserv.
3) Explore all the search options on Google, and make sure you're familiar with them.
4) Set up a Google news alert.
5) Google your name.

Listservs and newsgroups

You can join these in an area of interest, to look out for trends, tipoffs, ideas and contacts. Both involve people with a common interest (like the motor industry, for instance) exchanging news and views. With listservs, email messages are circulated to all members (check out a list at www.tile.net). With newsgroups, you go onto a site to read the postings (check out a list at www.cyberfiber.com).

Blogs

Weblogs are personal websites that people have set up as a kind of online diary. They post pictures, poetry or their thoughts on whatever concerns them, often adding links to other online material of relevance. They vary widely in quality – some are rubbish, others have become very influential. It all depends on whose blog it is. During the Iraq war, unique information on the situation in Baghdad came from bloggers in the city. The *Mail&Guardian* offers a facility for blogs – you can set up your own at www.blogmark.co.za.

The trouble with the Internet

The amazing size of the net can also be a great weakness. The volume of information can be simply unmanageable. If you ask Google to search for AIDS, for instance, you'll get over 200 million hits. That's too much to be of any use. You have to learn to search smartly, to limit the terms of the search using the search engine's grammar.

The other problem with the Internet is that any idiot can post material. You have to take at least as much care with checking the reliability of information you find online as with other sources. Ask yourself who is behind the site you have found. The World Bank? Well, then the information has the authority of the bank behind it (it could still be wrong). Joe Bloggs, 15, of Dakron, Ohio? Perhaps some caution is advised.

If a search has taken you directly to an inside page, look for a home button, or cut back the page's address to its stem so you can check the site out. It's also worth checking when the site was last updated – information may have been overtaken.

> ### CHECK IT OUT!
> - Gwen Ansell, Basic journalism. Milpark: M&G books, 2002. Ch 2 & 3
> - Francois Nel, Writing for the media in Southern Africa. Cape Town: Oxford University Press, 2005. Ch 6.
> - Andrew Boyd, Broadcast journalism. Oxford: Focal Press, 2002. Ch 3 & 4
> - Nora Paul: Computer-assisted research (posted at http://www.poynterextra.org/extra/newcar/index.html)
> - The Poynter Institute's collection of articles on writing and editing is at http://www.poynteronline.org/subject.asp?id=2
> - www.journalism.co.za has a substantial list of reporting resources, from online dictionaries to overseas databases. Look under 'Reporting tools'.

Filing your report

There are several different ways in which you can file your report. In later chapters, we will consider them in more detail.

Hard copy piece
This is a report consisting only of text, intended to be read by the newsreader. They are used in bulletins, often written off the wires when no sound is available.

Voicer
A voiced report from a journalist or correspondent, used in bulletins or news shows.

Clip, actuality or soundbite
A short piece of sound from a newsmaker, like a quote in newspaper copy, usually between 10 and 30 secs in length. Clips can be run on their own (as long as they are properly introduced), or embedded in a reporter's voicer.

It is difficult to file a clip from the field. For one thing, it is hard to edit sound on your recorder. Minidisk machines allow some editing, but it is laborious. You could find the beginning of the clip you want on your recorder, and then play it down the phone line (pause the tape at the right spot until the studio is ready to record.) But the quality is generally very poor.

Interview, Q&A or two-way
Interviews can be run as a conversation between presenter and interviewee either live or pre-recorded. If they are recorded for later broadcast, they can be edited to length.

Live crossing
If a journalist is on the scene of a news event, like a demonstration or a hostage crisis, she may report live by telephone. This is sometimes done during a bulletin, but not very often since they are very short. It is more common during a current affairs or other news show.

Tips for reporting on a shoestring

News on many community stations consists of stories lifted from the morning's newspapers, often without credit even being given to the paper. It is hard to do news where money is very tight, but just lifting stories really defeats the purpose of community radio. Here are some ideas for generating local story ideas on community stations:

- **Pay regular visits to all organisations active in the community:** Stay in touch with them, and make sure you know what they are busy with.
- **Invite guests to the studio:** If there's not enough money to do interviews in the field, ask local newsmakers into the studio to discuss an issue live. This could be a discussion with several participants, a phone-in programme or an interview with the host. Clips can be cut from such interviews and used in the bulletins.
- **Recording a taxi discussion:** It's technically a bit complex, but Katutura Community Radio in Namibia regularly records programmes in which taxi passengers debate the issues of the day, for later broadcast. It's called 'Kudu Express'.
- **Community helpline:** Jozi FM in Soweto runs an advice office where community people can get help on all kinds of issues. The office often produces ideas for news stories.
- **Local angles on national (or international) stories:** There are often easy ways of localising national stories. The Minister of Health has announced a new phase in the roll-out of antiretroviral drugs – why not find out what's happening at the local hospital? The Constitutional Court has made a ruling on land rights – why not ask the local farmers' association and farmworkers' union what they think? There's been a hurricane in the US – let's see whether the local churches are collecting aid.

You can also put somebody on air by simply handing your phone to them, and letting them talk to the presenter. A live interview with a demonstrator on the scene can make for powerful radio, since there will also be sound from the scene in the background, and s/he may be very emotional about whatever issue it is.

Package
When a reporter writes a script around the sound he has gathered, using different voices in addition to his own, we refer to the product as a news or feature package. It may include natural sound, and run for between two and five minutes. They are used in current affairs shows.

Documentary
Longer packages are known as documentaries. They are rare on South African radio.

1 Francois Nel, *Writing for the Media in Southern Africa*. Cape Town: Oxford University Press, 2005. p 122.
2 Franz Krüger, *Black, White and Grey: Ethics in SA journalism*. Cape Town: Double Storey,2004. p 183.

Journalists hard at work in the newsroom of Talk Radio 702

Chapter **4**

Writing for the ear

'Writing for radio is the storage of talk,' writes Robert McLeish. 'Presentation of a script at the microphone is the retrieval of that talk out of storage. The overall process should give the listener the impression that the broadcaster is talking to him rather than reading at him.'[1]

In fact, writing is not very good at storing the spoken word. When people speak, there is meaning in much more than the words they use. They use rhythm, pace and pauses; they emphasise some things by speaking more loudly or more emphatically. Take the sentence: 'You mean I have to be there at ten tomorrow.' It could have eight meanings, depending on whether I, there, ten, tomorrow or other words are stressed.[2] If you say the sentence out loud with the emphasis in different places, you will hear the different meanings.

Much radio is unscripted. When the presenter arrives in the studio, she simply

THE LEARNING CURVE

Hard to Listen

Liz picked up a stack of new faxes off the machine, and took one out. 'Here's something. Do you think you're up to doing a voicer from this?' she asked Ace.

Gratefully, he found a terminal and studied the statement. It was from the police: they had caught somebody doing 227 km/h on the highway – the fastest ever. It would be his first voicer for Sandi FM and he didn't want to mess it up.

He threw himself at the task, and finally had something he thought he could show Liz. She made a few small changes. 'Remember to keep those sentences short. And when the cops say radar speed detector, just call it a speed trap. But not bad, Ace. Liked your ending. We don't usually do this kind of thing, but it works here,' she said. 'You can record it'

He kept fluffing, but after four attempts, he had a clean recording. It was just before 5pm, and Liz smiled at him: 'We'll use it in the next bulletin, thanks. And I think its enough for the day.'

Ace rushed home. He lived with his granny, and he wanted to find out whether she'd heard. As he walked in, she said: 'I heard you on the radio! I was so proud, my boy.'

It was great to be able to share this triumph. 'Did you hear how I ended? 'Police would not say whether the speed trap would get counselling for shock'.'

'Eh?' his granny said uncertainly. 'Well, I know it was about the police, and a car. The kettle was boiling ... ' Brightening, she added: 'But your voice sounded very good.'

sits down and talks. Some kinds of radio format, like phone-in shows, can't be scripted in detail, although they should always be planned. Live interviews with a reporter on the scene, too, can't be scripted – they would just sound stiff, and lose the sense of immediacy. But they do run more smoothly if both interviewer and interviewee know what ground needs to be covered.

Some kinds of radio can't do without scripts. News bulletin items have to cram a lot of information into just a few seconds, and writing them beforehand means:

- you can be sure of covering all the important information
- you won't waste time stumbling over the words
- you won't get muddled, and the material will be presented logically and clearly
- somebody else can read the item a reporter has researched.

Writing a radio script is a skill that needs to be learned. We speak differently from the way we usually write. When we sit down with a pen and paper, or at a keyboard, we immediately adopt the habits of writing – our sentences are longer and more intricate. There are some words we would not think of using in writing, and others that we use even though we would not use them when we speak. When we write for radio, we have to unlearn those habits, and go back to oral forms.

Listeners are busy people. They may be driving, cooking, dealing with the children's homework or any number of other things. They are not concentrating on the radio, and that means we have to be very, very clear and simple. A radio journalist has only one chance to be understood. If the story is unclear, the chance has been wasted.

Get your head in gear

As with all writing, it is important to know exactly what the point, or the focus, of the story is. It will help you arrange the material and decide where the emphasis belongs. The focus will usually dictate the intro you write. Sometimes, there are two or even more possible news points: the police have found the body of a missing child, and residents have held a protest march about the disappearance. Usually, it is best to choose one aspect of the story as the main focus – unless you can write a simple sentence that covers both. You can always switch the angles around for a later bulletin.

Imagine you are addressing one person, not a crowd. 'Images of a sea of upturned faces somewhere beyond the studio lead only to megaphone newsreading and a style of writing which turns every story into a proclamation,' writes Andrew Boyd.[3] Avoid phrases like 'some of you' and 'listeners will know' – rather speak to one person.

You need to visualise a person to speak to – somebody who belongs to your target audience, preferably somebody you know. It will help you use the language and approach that make sense to your listeners.

It's a very good idea to write aloud – say the words as you put them down. It will help you write for the ear.

Once you are happy with your script, it needs to be edited. A second set of eyes may often spot possible improvements – or outright mistakes. The news editor should do this as a matter of course.

And rehearse any script before going live. You'll be more relaxed, present more smoothly and might even spot some problems.

The mechanics

If you're going to read the script from paper, you should make sure it is easy to read professionally.

Make your script easy to read
Use letters that are large enough, and leave enough space between lines. If you are writing by hand, make sure you write neatly.

Type in upper and lower case
Some older books recommend that you type in capitals, but in fact normal sentence case (like this) is easier on the eye. Some people have got used to reading capitals, and then of course it's better to stick with what you are used to.

Type on one side of the paper only
Turning a page over can make a noise.

Don't allow a paragraph to run onto the next page, or break a word between lines
It's harder to read.

Be careful to spell correctly
Mistakes can trip the reader up. Try to read the following sentence correctly: Predisent Thabo Mabeli sayshe wilnothesitate to act agianst any party o ffic ial fundto be corrupt. See?

Help with difficult pronunciation
You can indicate the pronunciation in brackets behind the word.

Put hyphens between the letters of an acronym
Write U-S-A: it is easier to read.

Show emphasis and pauses
A set of dots in the middle of the sentence can be used to indicate where the reader should pause. Underline words (or parts of words) that need emphasis.

If you are reading straight off computer, most of these rules apply, too. Many adjustments can be made by setting the screen correctly.

Principles

Use conversational language
Write like people talk. It is perfectly acceptable to use contractions like wouldn't, he's, won't etc. It does not mean they have to be used in every case: sometimes the full form is better, for the sake of clarity or emphasis. However, we should be careful of slang. In newswriting, people expect a slightly more formal language than in other areas, and some words and expressions would seem out of place. Think of it as a reasonably polite conversation at the dinner table.

Well-written radio news will reflect the patterns and rhythms of the way people in South Africa actually speak. In whatever language we broadcast, we should be trying to write and speak it well. This does not mean sacrosanct, pretentious, in-a-glass-case language. It does mean clear, uncluttered and accessible language.
– SABC Radio News styleguide

RADIO

Vigorous writing is concise. A sentence should contain no unnecessary words, for the same reason that a drawing should have no unnecessary lines and a machine no unnecessary parts. This requires not that the writer make all his sentences short, or that he avoid all detail and treat his subjects only in outline, but that every word tell. – William Strunk Jr & E.B. White[4]

Use simple, clear, direct language

Use short, plain words rather than long, complex ones, and see whether you can replace a phrase with a single word. 'Ask' is better than 'request'; 'end' is better than 'terminate'; 'try' is better than 'attempt'. E. Joseph Broussard and Jack F. Holgate write: 'Replace those elegant fifty cent words with simple ten cent ones which nearly everyone can understand.'[5] Abstract words are harder to visualise than concrete ones – radio is about getting people to create pictures in their imaginations, and it's easier to conjure up the picture of a fire than a conflagration.

Avoid jargon

Bureaucrats and specialists of various kinds use particular words that outsiders don't always understand. Journalists need to ask themselves: what does this mean, how can I translate this into normal language so that my listeners will understand what is going on? It's not good enough to say, as some journalists do: well, I don't understand it, but it's what she said. If you don't understand it, the chances are your listeners won't either.

Avoid clichés

Expressions like 'last-ditch attempt', 'meets the eye', 'final analysis' and many others are just tired, and should be allowed some well-deserved rest. It is better to look for an original, direct and preferably simple way of expressing the idea.

Choose simple, direct sentences

The best sentence structure is the simple form of subject – verb – object, eg the car hit the man. These are the easiest to understand. Sentences that begin with a long qualifying clause are hard to follow, because they keep listeners waiting a long time for the main part of the sentence. Shorter ones can sometimes be used, but try to read this sentence: In a last-ditch attempt to pull his party back from the brink of a long-threatening oblivion due to the steady losses from floor-crossing, the Independence Party's Joe Bloggs has gone to court to challenge the latest defections. Even worse are sentences that push the subject and the verb apart, by inserting qualifying material of that kind. (In that terrible sentence about Joe Bloggs, try to move the long piece at the beginning – 'in a last ditch … from floor-crossing' – to just after Bloggs: it becomes even harder to follow.) Keep the subject near the action.

Vary the lengths of sentences, but prefer shorter ones

In general, shorter sentences are better. A good rule of thumb is to use one idea per sentence. But be careful of becoming monotonous. Vary the lengths of sentences to improve the rhythm.

Space the information

Don't overload sentences with facts and detail, they can become too dense and hard to understand. Choose the really important stuff, and space it so that people have a little bit of time to 'chew on' something heavy, like a statistic or a complicated idea, before they are hit with the next one.

Attribution

As with all journalism, radio reports need to indicate where the information comes from. It helps listeners judge its value, and places the responsibility for it squarely on the source. 'The police say that six people died in the taxi accident.' The more controversial the claim is, the more important it is to be clear about where it comes from. Unlike print, however, radio reports usually put the source first. We don't say, 'Six people died in the taxi accident, police say.'

Quotations

People can't hear quote marks, so it's generally better to use indirect speech if you don't have tape of the quote you want to use. When the words are particularly striking, you can indicate that it is a quote by using a phrase like 'in his words', or 'as she put it'. The reader can indicate the quoted words by making a short pause and changing the tone of the voice slightly. Avoid the phrase 'quote, unquote'.

Use the active voice

It is usually better to say 'the dog bit the child' (active) than 'the child was bitten by the dog'.

Abbreviations and acronyms

An abbreviation is the shortened form of a word, like Mr for Mister. Journalists often deal with the abbreviated names of organisations – the United Democratic Movement, for instance, is also known as the UDM. When an abbreviation can be read as a word, like Unisa, or AIDS, it is known as an acronym. They pose particular difficulties for radio because they can be unfamiliar to listeners, confusing and can make newsreaders stumble. The basic rule is to avoid them if possible. However, where an abbreviation is very well known – like ANC – it can be used freely, and does not need to be spelled out. Where the organisation is less well known, it is best to give the full name the first time it comes up, and then refer to it as 'the union' or 'the group'. Remember that you may be very used to dealing with the South African Democratic Teachers' Union, and refer to it as SADTU all the time, but your listeners may not be. Always make quite sure there can be no doubt about who you are referring to.

Titles

Some government and company officials have the most amazing job titles. There are two problems with them – they can be very long, taking up precious radio time, and they can be full of jargon, and people just can't understand what they mean. As long as you remain accurate, it's perfectly acceptable to simplify titles. Let's say you are dealing with Nosimo Vilakazi, whose proper title is deputy director: product development and marketing strategy. You could easily refer to her as Nosimo Vilakazi, who's in charge of new products, or even just as 'senior company official'.

Tenses

Radio is about what's happening now, not what happened last week. So it's best to use various forms of the present tense: the simple present – 'the police say'; the present progressive – 'the police are saying'; or the present perfect – 'the police have said'. Where possible, we should stay with the simple present: 'The mayor says he won't put up with inefficiency.' If it's important to indicate when he spoke (at a public meeting last night, eg), then we have to move into the past tense.

Usually, if the story happened yesterday, it's best to leave out the time reference. We shouldn't usually be writing stories about things that happened so long ago.

Numbers

A stream of numbers is very hard to absorb. Long economic stories packed with statistics are usually just noise – nobody remembers what they say. Choose just the most important ones, and make it clear what their significance is. If you report that 'car prices have gone up 20% in the last year', it can be just a number. But if you say: 'A new car will cost you 20% more than last year,' the relevance will immediately be clear to the listener. Also, you should round numbers up or down. It makes more sense to talk about a company losing 'almost R2 million' in a cash robbery, than to give the exact figure of R1 927 034.27.

Intros

We follow the general journalistic convention of writing an intro that focuses on the most important aspect of the story. Usually, a radio intro is a little longer than one in print, running to more than one sentence, particularly when it introduces a voicer or a feature package. The opening sentence of an intro needs to be short and sharp – but remember that listeners take a moment or two to warm up, to 'tune into' the subject matter of the story. So it's not a good idea to launch in with an unfamiliar name or title – it will leave listeners wondering who the person is, and their attention won't stay with you as you develop the story. (There are particular issues that arise when we introduce a clip, voice report or the like, and these will be dealt with in Chapter 6.)

Endings

The ends of stories are important in radio, because that's what stays with the listener. Radio stories should never be structured as an inverted pyramid. They should keep listeners' interest throughout, right until the end. With radio, once somebody's attention has wandered, it's unlikely to come back easily. The last sentence must be strong, but avoid clichés like 'time will tell whether residents' fears will be addressed,' or the like.

Tips for writing on a shoestring

The writing tips above don't depend on whether you have money or not. If you don't have a computer, you should still try to write news stories and other scripts before going on air. If you are writing by hand, make sure the story is easy to read – the writing must be clear and there should not be too many corrections. If you find yourself crossing out a lot of material, it may be better to start again on a clean sheet of paper.

The tips here are based on English practice. Sentence structure, clichés and other issues may be quite different in other languages. We can't address all these issues of usage here – but the basic point remains the same: what you say must be clear and easy to understand.

Write for the mind

Radio is actually a very visual medium – it can create pictures in the mind. Even short news items benefit from a little bit of descriptive writing. 'The accused tugged at his string tie as he pleaded not guilty' gives listeners a picture of the man. But it needs to be real and vivid – people too often just use clichés – the anxious mother waiting for news, the furious mob. Strong, visual nouns and verbs are the best tools – adverbs should be avoided, and adjectives used sparingly.

Tone

This needs to match the subject matter of the story. If it's a funny story, the tone should be light; if it's tragic, you have to be serious.

Ambiguities

Be careful about writing things that can mean something quite different from what you intended. If you read a sentence like 'Golfer Ernie Els was playing a round with his wife,' your listeners are likely to have a good laugh at your expense.

Repeating words or phrases

Try to avoid using the same word repeatedly. If you've referred to an 'organisation', it could easily become a 'group' at the next mention.

Note

These tips are meant as guidelines. In the end, there is only one test: is the story clear and easy to understand? Sometimes, you will need to break a rule in order

DO IT!

1) Improve the following sentences, to make them suitable for a radio report. Look particularly for ways of making them simpler and more direct.
   a. The building was completely destroyed.
   b. Criminal activity in suburban areas without blockwatch systems in place can at this point in time not be said to be noticeably higher than those in areas with such systems.
   c. Even though there were 21 000 fewer people with jobs – because there were more new entrants to the job market than jobs created, the 1.9% increase in jobs in the South African economy between April and June reflects a sharp turnaround from the previous quarter, when the number of jobs declines 2.1%.
   d. In a written reply to a parliamentary question from the Democratic Alliance yesterday, the Minister of Home Affairs, Nosiviwe Mapisa-Nqakula, confirmed that no investigation had taken place into the issuing of a false passport to US actor Wesley Snipes and said that the passport had not been issued by the department or any departmental official.
   e. The clinic's chief director of clinical and nursing services, Dr Henrietta Van Schalkwyk, said the accident victims are resting comfortably.
   f. The court was surrounded by an angry crowd, who demanded justice for the alleged rapist.
   g. Sadtu says its members won't accept the pay increase. Sadtu's general secretary David Smith says, and I quote, 'We won't accept the offer.' He added that Sadtu's negotiating team is unhappy with the attitude of the employers, and that Sadtu will be considering its options going forward.

2) Write an intro for a news story based on the following facts:
   a. Ms Lerato Motswenyane, 24.
   b. Teacher at Ikhwezi Senior Secondary School, Pimville.
   c. Dead of apparent strangulation.
   d. Found 2:30am today in an open field near the school.
   e. Found by an unnamed man on his way to work
   f. She taught English and home economics.
   g. She is married, with two children of 5 and 2 years.
   h. Post mortem investigations are being conducted, to check whether she was raped.
   i. Police are investigating.

3) Write a 40-second bulletin item based on the following facts:
   A 21-year-old mother lives with her little sister (four years old) and her baby girl of one month in a house in Kensington, Johannesburg. She lives there with 15 other people. They are squatting in the house, and water and electricity have been cut off. Neighbours have often complained to health authorities and the owner about the house. They say there is a lot of noise. There is also often a stench of sewage coming from it.
   Earlier today, the mother left her baby and her little sister alone in their room. It was a cold morning, and she left a paraffin stove on to keep them warm.
   Wili Nxumalo and her husband Zakes also live there. Wili Nxumalo was in the kitchen washing dishes when she heard the four-year-old scream. There was smoke everywhere in the house. She ran out of the house. The four-year-old also ran out. There was fire everywhere. She said the baby was already unconscious from the smoke.
   Emergency services came after about 30 minutes. The firemen put out the fire. The woman's room was very badly damaged. They found the baby was dead. The mother arrived back soon after the firemen had put out the fire. She was terribly upset. A minister who works with the emergency services, Rev Horace McBride, comforted her.
   Later, doctors carried out a post mortem. They found that the baby did not die from the fire, but from breathing in smoke.
   At a press conference this afternoon, a police spokesperson said an inquest docket had been opened. They wanted to make sure what caused the fire.

to make something clear. As George Orwell said, 'Break any of these rules sooner than say something outright barbarous.'[6]

1 Roberr McLeish, *Radio Production*. Oxford: Focal Press, 1998. p 61
2 Ibid, 62
3 Andrew Boyd, *Broadcast Journalism: Techniques for Radio and Television News*. Oxford: Focal Press, 2002. p 58
4 William Strunk Jr & E.B. White, *The Elements of Style*. Boston: Allyn & Bacon, 1979. 23.
5 E. Joseph Broussard & Jack F. Holgate, *Writing and Reporting Broadcast News*. New York: Macmillan Publishing Co, 1982. p 51
6 George Orwell, *Why I Write*. London: Penguin, 1984. p 119

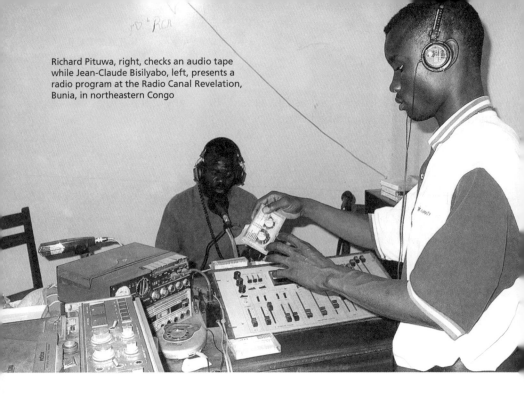

Richard Pituwa, right, checks an audio tape
while Jean-Claude Bisilyabo, left, presents a
radio program at the Radio Canal Revelation,
Bunia, in northeastern Congo

Chapter **5**

Equipment 1: Recorders

Although the available recording equipment has changed dramatically, all
machines have to deal with the same physical properties of sound. It is useful to
understand some of these basic principles.

Sound consists of vibrations passing through the air. The sound of hands
clapping, for instance, travels like a wave in water, reaching our eardrum and
causing it to vibrate. Messages are sent to our brain, which hears the clap.

The faster the air vibrates, the higher the sound is. We talk of the frequency
of the sound, and measure it in hertz. The highest sounds humans can hear
measure around 6000 hertz, or 6 kilohertz (kHz); the lowest measure around
16Hz. Many animals can hear sounds outside this range.

The volume of sound is measured in decibels (dB). If sound is very loud, like a
gunshot (around 130 dB), it can cause us pain.

THE LEARNING CURVE

The Pause Button

When the call from the police came, Ace was the only one in the office. They had made further arrests in the case of the rape of the little girls. Liz said: 'Do you think you can manage? Just get the cops on tape, and bring it back. We'll work out what to do with it then. You do know how to operate a Minidisk? They do teach you that at tech?'

Ace Reporter, he thought, as he dashed off. He would show her he could do the job.

An hour later, he was back from police headquarters, and swung the minidisk proudly onto Liz's desk. 'It was good. They have arrested three more people as accomplices. They'll be in court tomorrow.

'Let's see what you've got,' she said, and pressed play.

Nothing.

She glanced up at him. 'And now?'

'It's there, I know it,' he said, with a sinking feeling. 'It was really strong stuff.'

Liz picked up the recorder and examined it. 'You'll find you record better when you don't leave the pause button on. You'd better write it hard.'

She turned to Thatho. 'We don't have sound on this kids rape story. Can you line up the cops for the show later? At least we can do it that way.'

Ace Reporter, he thought bitterly.

In this chapter, we will discuss recording techniques. Later on, we will consider how to use and edit sound.

Microphones

Microphones convert sound into an electrical signal. In a public address system, the signal is boosted and then turned back into sound over a loudspeaker. In recording equipment, the signal is stored for later use. There are different kinds of microphones, which all have particular strengths and weaknesses. It is important to choose the right microphone for the task at hand, although most radio reporters will make do with a single multi-purpose mike.

A moving coil, or dynamic mike

This has a wire coil attached to a diaphragm. The sound makes the diaphragm and the coil vibrate, which generates a variable electric charge because it is situated inside a magnetic field. These mikes need no power supply, which means you don't have to worry about batteries or cords but also that their output is softer. They are less sensitive to interference from cellphones and radios and are usually robust. They are widely used as field microphones.

> In my opinion, the most dangerous machine of them all is the microphone. – BBC presenter Esther Rantzen[1]

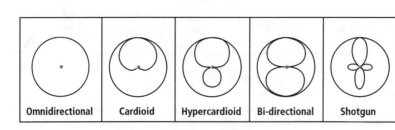

Pickup patterns of different mikes

| Omnidirectional | Cardioid | Hypercardioid | Bi-directional | Shotgun |

A condenser mike

This has an electrically charged capacitor in place of the diaphragm. It can't work without electric current, but the quality of sound is very high. These mikes are more sensitive, and are often used in studios.

Microphones also differ in their pick-up (directivity) pattern – their efficiency in picking up sound from different patterns.

Omni-directional mikes

They record evenly from all sides. They are versatile in that they are not as sensitive to exact handling, but they can also sometimes pick up unwanted background noise. They are useful for recording ambient sound.

Uni-directional mikes

These pick up sound much better from the front than the back. Because the pick-up pattern is heart-shaped, they are also known as cardioid mikes. They are used when unwanted noise needs to be suppressed.

Bi-directional mikes

These microphones pick up sound in a figure-of-eight pattern, and are useful for recording two sources which are facing each other, as long as they don't move around. This kind of mike is not so common.

Shotgun mikes

They are extremely uni-directional. They are often used by TV crews, and are useful for 'cutting through' background noise, such as when you find yourself at the back of a crowded news conference.

Whatever mike you use, a popshield or windshield is an important accessory. It is a small piece of foam that fits over the mike, and it helps eliminate windnoise and the explosive 'p' that some people seem to produce when they speak.

Recording equipment

Digital technologies have changed the way radio reporters work. Where they used to carry around huge reel-to-reel machines, they now have a range of different kinds of machines to choose from.

Cassette recorders

Reel-to-reel recorders were replaced by smaller and more convenient cassette recorders. There is a huge difference in quality between recorders that are aimed at the general consumer market, and those that professionals use. Cassette recorders store sound magnetically on tape. Good makes used by journalists include Marantz and Sony.

MiniDisk recorders

These save the sound digitally on a small magneto-optical disc, which has space for up to 148 minutes of mono recording. Digital technology allows for better sound quality than analogue systems, it is generally cheaper and machines are smaller. The MD machines are shock-proof because they store several seconds of recording in RAM memory. Users have instant access to various tracks, and can edit the sound on the recorder itself, although this is awkward.

The minidisk's humble 'End search' button: a powerful friend

After a disk has been put in, any recording will begin at the start of the disk. If there is something already there, it will simply record over the existing material. Many precious interviews have been lost in this way. But a little button will take the machine to the end of all material already on the disk, and start from there. It's called the 'end search' button – and it is a powerful ally. It is a good idea to get into the habit of ALWAYS pressing it before a recording, just to make sure you don't record over anything.

DAT machines

They use digital audiocassettes that are no bigger than a stamp, and allow different tracks to be accessed almost as quickly as on the MiniDisc. They have not really taken hold in radio journalism.

Solid-state recorders

Just like computers, these machines work with built in microchip memory. A small LCD screen allows editing in the field, and a special interface allows reports to be sent back to the studio using a special, high-quality digital phone line. There are no moving parts and no motor, which makes them very robust. They were costly, but prices are coming down, and they are likely to become the new standard.

Dictaphones

Some smaller stations use Dictaphones. They usually record onto cassettes, although newer models have a digital memory. They cost much less than other machines, but deliver poor audio quality.

What the buttons do

Most recorders have similar core functions. Whatever machine you use, you should become completely familiar with it. Make sure you work through the manual in detail, and become thoroughly comfortable with it before you set out on your first assignment. You don't want to be struggling with the buttons when you're doing a real interview.

What can go wrong:
(Examples of most of these problems can be found on the CD included with this book)

Cable Sound: A severe distortion or a loud rough, beating sound, usually caused by a damaged cable or component. It can also be caused by the cable rubbing against the mike casing.
Solution: check your cable, or hold it very still.
Crackling: An irregular form of very light static, similar to the sound a fire makes, often caused by poor cable or other electrical connections. Other causes are electrical interference or a defective power supply on the phone.
Solution: check your connections.
Crosstalk is when you can hear someone else's conversation on a telephone.
Solution: put down the phone, and dial again, preferably on a landline.
Echo is when the talker hears his or her own voice fed back, especially when conducting telephone interviews. The term is also used for the echo that arises when interviewing in a very large space, like a hall.
Solution: Put down the phone and dial again, preferably on a landline. For the other kind of echo, move to another location.
Fluctuating voice is when the volume of the voice increases and decreases like a wave. It is usually caused by the speaker swaying towards and away from the microphone.
Solution: get the speaker to stand still.
Fuzzy voice, or distorted sound is like a radio being played too loud.
Solution: turn the levels on the recorder down.
Hissing is a driven white noise that overwhelms the voice. Hissing is more driven and constant than static. White noise is a term often associated with strong hissing. Pink noise is a less constant hissing noise and brown noise even less constant still. It is often caused by using a tape that has been overused.
Solution: Use a new, high quality tape.
Humming is a buzzing noise of interference from an electromagnetic source. An example is the sound heard on a radio when a nearby mobile phone is about to be called or detecting a cell.
Solution: move away from the source of the noise, or turn off the cellphone.
Muffled Voice sounds similar to speaking with your hand over your mouth. It is usually caused by incorrect tone settings on the recorder.
Solution: check the tone settings.
Popping: When you hold the microphone too close to somebody's mouth, sometimes t's and p's are recorded as little pops.
Solution: Move the mike, or use a popshield (a piece of foam that fits over the mike)
Soft voice is usually caused by a volume setting that is too low.
Solution: get the speaker to speak more loudly, move closer with your mike or set the volume higher.
Static is a granular distortion similar to bad reception on the radio. This is also often caused by electrical interference.
Solution: move away from the likely source of interference, or switch it off.
Howlaround, or feedback: When the mike picks up the sound it has just recorded coming out of a loudspeaker, it creates a terrible noise.
Solution: Turn the monitor off.
Wind noise is when the mike records a low whooshing from the wind.
Solution: Use a popshield or go indoors.

Levels should always be even – in other words all voices should be recorded at similar levels.

(With thanks to Mosotho Stone)

All recorders have the same play, pause, fast forward and rewind buttons that are familiar on entertainment units, as well as volume controls. They must have the capacity to record. Some have inbuilt mikes, but these are rarely good enough for professional use.

You will listen to the sound either over an inbuilt speaker or over earphones. Some machines allow you to listen either off the source or off the tape, which is a useful function. It is possible to hear the sound even if it is not recording. If you switch to listening off tape, you will hear only what is being recorded. In this way you can make sure that what you are hearing is actually on the tape.

> One problem with the hand-held mike is that the user needs to invade the other person's physical space to get a decent signal. In body language terms, this invasion of space normally takes place only when people are fighting or being intimate, so expect some natural apprehension on the part of the interviewee and to feel uncomfortable yourself at first. At this point, plenty of confidence, a little charm, a ready smile, well-brushed teeth and a good deodorant are the reporter's most valuable assets.
> – Andrew Boyd[2]

The counter on a cassette machine is an important feature. It allows you to keep track of your material, and find the part you want quickly. MD machines keep track of the time during recording, and allow you to mark tracks on the disk.

A level indicator shows the volume of recording, and takes the form either of a VU meter – a gauge with a needle – or an LCD display. If the levels are too low, the recording may be too soft to hear, and if they are too high, it may distort.

In addition, the device will have jacks for a microphone, power, line input and output and some others. More sophisticated ones include controls to change various aspects of recording or playback.

Recording techniques

Check the equipment
Before you start, it is important to check that everything is in working order. Make sure the batteries aren't flat, that you have spares and that you have enough space to record, whether you're using cassettes, minidiscs or anything else. It is a good idea to do a short test recording.

The setting
The surroundings make a huge difference to the sound quality. It is best to minimise these problems at the time of the interview – some of them can create big problems during editing.

A room with too many hard surfaces creates an echo and can make the recording sound like it was done in a bathroom. If you're inside, it is best to look for an environment with curtains, carpets on the floor and soft furniture.

Then there's background noise. Sometimes, the background adds authenticity – the noise of a taxi rank, for instance, helps listeners put themselves at the scene. But it must not be allowed to overwhelm the interview. If the situation is very noisy, it may be necessary to find a quieter spot – a side street, for instance. Sometimes, sitting inside a car offers a solution.

We tend to screen out some kinds of noise. We don't notice a ticking clock, or standard office noises like an air conditioner or the hum of a computer, but the mike will pick them up quite clearly and they will be distracting during broadcast. Listen for these kinds of noise, and ask for equipment to be switched off. You can also ask for the phone to be taken off the hook so that it can't ring.

A noisy street can be blocked off by closing a window, or even the curtains, too.

Cellphones and other equipment can cause electronic interference, another reason to ask for them to be switched off. You will hear this very clearly if you are listening on headphones.

Background music can be very difficult, since it will be impossible to edit the interview without the music being chopped up. If you need the music for ambience, it is best to do the interview in a quiet place, record the music separately and then lay it down as a track once you've edited the interview.

Intermittent noise is the most difficult to deal with. If you're close to an airport, you can be sure that the aircraft will be taking off in the middle of your interviewee's most striking comment. There's not much you can do except try to get them to repeat themselves, or pause when you hear an aircraft approaching. Both options are very disruptive to the flow of the interview, though.

If all else fails – and there are situations where you can't sort out a noise problem – use close mike work. Bringing the microphone closer in blocks out some background noise – but you will have to be careful of popping.

Sitting comfortably

It is important to arrange your interviewee in a comfortable position for recording. Try not to do the interview across somebody's huge wooden desk. The polished surface of the desk will create an echo, and you're going to get a very tired arm stretching the mike across, particularly if the person leans back comfortably in their office chair.

DO IT!

Do it!

1) Do a range of different recordings of short (2-3 minute) interviews. Use these and other settings:
   - In a bathroom
   - In an office
   - On a taxi rank
   - On a construction site
   - Outside, on a windy day

Play back the interviews. Are they clear? Experiment with different techniques to make the interviews sound as clear as possible.

2) Roleplay an interview with a colleague. Choose a subject to discuss, and record yourselves. Ask your partner to do things like shuffling, leaning suddenly away from the mike, coughing etc, and see how well you cope.

Standing together is a good option, although for many people it will feel odd to do so in an office. Sitting next to each other in an L shape works very well. It brings you close enough while feeling natural. And it you will be able to reach with your mike without your arm getting too tired.

You may also have to deal with an interviewee who has clinking jewellery, or the habit of constantly clicking a pen. It is best to ask the person politely to put them aside for the moment. A little joke can work wonders.

Tips for recording sound on a shoestring

Try to get at least one recorder of reasonable quality. While cassette dictaphones are much cheaper than other equipment, the sound quality is really not good enough for broadcast. The new solid state dictaphones are better. If possible invest in a microphone, at least. You will get much better quality if you use a separate mike than if you use the in-built one.

Handling the mike

Grip your mike firmly but not tightly. Also make sure that any ring you might be wearing does not rub against it. It is best to loop the cable around your hand, keeping it away from the mike casing with your fingers. But don't stretch it tightly; this can pull against the jack that is plugged into the recorder, causing damage. Cables can make a lot of noise, and need careful handling.

A mike should usually be held around 20cm from the interviewee's mouth – about the distance between your outstretched thumb and little finger. Hold it slightly below the person's mouth – it takes it out of their immediate line of vision (which is less threatening), and minimises the dangers of popping.

Don't hand over your mike to the interviewee. There's a good chance she will mishandle it, causing noise you don't want on the recording. Even more importantly, the mike is the key to control of the interview. And you should always remain in control.

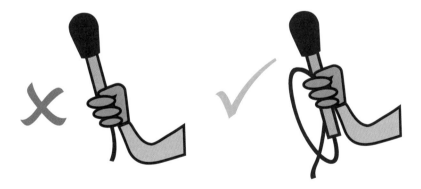

Checking levels

With digital editing equipment, you can easily make adjustments to the levels while editing. But it is still better to record at the right levels. You do this by setting the levels at the beginning of the interview. Make sure you are sitting in the position you will keep for the interview, and then record a sentence or two. It is a good idea to use a question that is unconnected to the interview: it breaks the ice, relaxes the interviewee and you don't risk getting the best line of the interview before you've begun, and while your settings still need adjusting. You can change the settings on the recorder, or adjust the distance of the mike. It rarely helps to ask somebody to speak louder – inevitably, they will forget after the first sentence, and you're back where you started.

Many recorders have automatic level control functions. These boost the volume when it drops too low, and cut it when it goes too high. It sounds fantastic, but it has some real drawbacks. It means you have reduced control over the sound quality. Also, the system sometimes pumps up background noise when the speaker makes a pause, and this can be very distracting.

A natural conversation

With all these technical considerations, it is difficult to make the conversation natural. But it is important to try. If you're forever checking the questions in your notebook, twiddling with the equipment or glancing at the tape counter, it can be very disconcerting for the interviewee. Eye contact is important, you need to respond to the normal conversational cues from her and give your own when necessary. Of course, it is better to nod than to say anything that you might have to edit out later.

Finishing

When you're done, check that the recording is on the tape. It is better to do a quick retake right away than to have to come back at another time. Check the person's title and name, including the pronunciation. It's good to check the spelling, too. It may not seem important, but a newsreader may mispronounce a name if it is misspelled.

People will often want to know when the item will be aired. It is fine to indicate when it is intended for, but newsrooms are unpredictable places, and all kinds of things can happen. It is important not to make definite promises.

1 Quoted in Andrew Boyd, *Broadcast Journalism*. Oxford: Focal Press, 2002. 248
2 Boyd, op cit, 254

Chapter **6**

Making sound bite

Radio is about sound. The SABC's radio news manual says: 'Print journalists use photos to enhance their stories, TV journalists use footage. Radio journalists use sound to paint pictures in the minds of their listeners or to make them think. Sound provides the colour and texture of your story. But it doesn't begin and end only with words and speech. It can also include silences and pauses, ambience, sound fx, and appropriate music.'[1]

We use the recorded words of somebody involved in a story because they add authority and often colour to the report. When the Zimbabwean President said some time ago: 'Let Tony Blair keep his Britain and let me keep my Zimbabwe!' the choice of words spoke volumes about Robert Mugabe and his mood of defiance, and newspapers used the quote prominently. The recording of him saying the words – available to radio – was even more striking: his well-known voice, his style

THE LEARNING CURVE

Live and Direct

It was mid-morning of day five in the Sandi FM newsroom for Ace. Suddenly, the door swung open and Lerato swept into the newsroom. She rushed up to the newsdesk, and consulted Liz. Seconds later, she was on her way again. 'Go with Lerato,' Liz called to Ace. 'Watch her. Don't get in the way.'

In the car, Lerato explained: residents of Luanda were demonstrating outside the municipal offices. They were really angry about the children who were in hospital after playing in dirty puddles in the street, and were demanding proper toilets.

'Your sanitation story is turning out to be quite a big one,' he said. 'Seems like it,' she said, looking pleased.

Outside the municipality, about 50 people were chanting slogans: 'No more buckets! Clean water is our right!' Lerato leapt out and began taping the chanting. She glanced at her watch: just about time for the bulletin. She drew one of the women aside, while dialling the office number on her cellphone.

Ace had the car radio on, and heard Liz's voice, introducing the 11am bulletin. 'A group of angry residents are protesting against poor sanitation outside the municipal offices. Our reporter Lerato Mofokeng is on the scene. Lerato, what's happening?' And then Lerato's fluent and confident voice, describing the scene and talking about sick children. 'With me is Lydia Jantjies, one of the protestors. Ma'm Lydia, what do residents want?'

And he could see her pass the phone to Jantjies, whose voice came over the car radio, strong and angry. 'They must do something. We are dying here. We are tired of promises. All these councillors can do is drive big cars and get fat with our money.' She was still talking, Ace could see, but Liz's voice was back on the radio. 'We'll keep you informed on this breaking story. In Cape Town, meanwhile ... '

On the street, Lerato got her phone back, brought out her Minidisk and mike instead, and recorded a few minutes of interview. Then she waved to Ace. 'I need to get the mayor,' and disappeared behind the glass door.

Not long afterwards, she was jumping back into the car with a grin. 'I think I've got everything for now.' She glanced at her watch. 'It would be nice to get the mayor into the next bulletin, but we won't be back in time. I'll see what Liz wants for 12.'

A quick call to the office, and Lerato was writing the script for a voice report in the notebook balanced on her knee. She filed it over the phone, and they were off. They had spent just under an hour there. It was wonderful to watch her work. At tech, he had admired her from afar, beautiful and distant. Now here he was in the car with her.

'You're amazing,' said Ace, not sure whether he meant the woman or the journalist.

'All in a day's work,' she said, smiling. 'They'll use my voicer in the next bulletin, then there's the clip of the mayor for the one afterwards, then we'll probably go back to Lydia. That was a great soundbite on air, I hope they taped it. She was really furious. Otherwise I'll get something off my interview, but it wasn't that strong. And I need to make a quick package for the show this evening. We'll probably need to set up a live interview for them too. Wonder who they will want.'

Ace was overwhelmed, but he didn't want to show it. After all, he was supposed to be impressing her. So he said nothing. They drove in silence.

of delivery illustrated the kind of man he was. And it said to listeners: this is real.

Similarly, the breaking voice of a grieving husband makes for powerful radio, allowing listeners to empathise in a way that is impossible in print. And the ambient sound from demonstrations or other events add a sense of authenticity to a report. It says the reporter was there, and could see what was going on.

But not all sound is created equal. Officials often say things that are fairly simple in a long and complicated way. There's no point in using clips of that kind – they take up time and confuse listeners. It's better to paraphrase.

Telling quotes and turns of phrase – like the line from Mugabe – make for powerful clips. Sound must make a contribution to your story – don't just put it in for its own sake.

How long? Each station has its own approach to lengths. But generally, voice reports don't run much longer than 50 secs, and a clip is between 10 and 25 secs.

Collecting sound

Many radio newsrooms rely very heavily on the telephone for collecting soundbites, because it's cheaper and quicker than going out on a story. As long as the phone line is clear and the technical quality good, that's fine. But recording somebody face-to-face will always give you better quality. The sound itself will be clearer, and the person will respond to you differently in person than on the other end of a phone line.

Keep an ear open for opportunities to record sound when you're out on a story. Try to get as close to the source of the sound as possible. If you're at a public meeting, recording the speaker from the back of the hall will be marginal, at best. Try to get your microphone onto the lectern, if possible, or do a one-on-one interview with the speaker afterwards, in which you ask him or her about the main points.

It is a good idea to wear your headphones while recording – it gives you a better idea of the sound quality, and helps you spot problems.

Handling clips in other languages:

Often, you will end up with sound in a language that is not your broadcast language. In some cases, you may be able to use the clip as it is, if you think your listeners will follow. English clips are often used on stations broadcasting in other languages, for instance, and Zulu listeners will have no difficulties with siSwati. If this is not possible, you should use a voice-over. Record a translation of the clip, and place it over the original in such a way that the original is heard briefly in the clear first, and is then dipped down very softly under the translation. The translation can be done on location or later in the studio. If you are interviewing somebody through an interpreter, you must make sure that you get both the original sound and the translation clearly and separately, or else editing will become quite difficult.

Another technique used on some stations is to run the clip, and then provide a brief summary in your broadcast language. This is quicker to do than recording a voice-over, but can sound clumsy

Writing a voicer

The basic rules of writing for radio have been covered in Chapter 4, and they apply to voicers as much as any other script.

A voicer can contain only the reporter's voice, or it can include ambient sound, or a clip, or both. Since bulletin items are short, there's not usually time for much more than a single clip. Longer feature packages will be discussed separately.

It is not a good idea to begin a voicer with a clip, because it makes it difficult to introduce the item. The newsreader has to name both voices: the reporter's and the newsmaker's, and this can be confusing. It is better for the cue to set up the reporter, who hands on to the newsmaker, and then comes back in to finish the report.

However, you can start a report with a brief burst of the sound, and then dip it under your voice.

Radio stations usually have a particular style for the reporter to sign off at the end. The standard outcue (SOQ) usually gives the reporter's name, where he or she is reporting from, and the station or programme name. An example might be 'This is Ace Tshabalala, Sandi FM, Mdantsane.' In general, the simpler the SOQ is, the better.

> ### Tips for getting sound on a shoestring
>
> Even the most cash-strapped station should make telephones and field recorders available to get some real sound into the news. If necessary, a recorder can be shared and a phone can be strictly controlled.
>
> Reporting from the scene will automatically give you the background sound and feel of the event, adding to the authenticity of the report. This can be done before the bulletin, if the news producer has time to do a bit of editing, or live, if you prepare very carefully what you want to say. It is best to work with a script for a bulletin contribution, but in a longer news show, a Q&A with prepared questions works best.
>
> You can get extra sound by handing your phone to somebody who's involved in the story: a striking worker, for instance. The host back in the studio can do the interview live, and a clip can be cut for use in a later bulletin.

Writing a cue

Any voicer from a reporter or a clip from a newsmaker needs to be introduced properly with a cue. For the listener, there is no real distinction – they hear the two as one, which means they must fit well together. It is usually best for the reporter to write the cue, too, to avoid duplication or other problems. Somebody else can only write it if he or she knows exactly what's in the bite or voicer.

Radio cues can be a little longer than intros in print. Two reasonably short sentences, or three to four lines, are about right. If a cue is too short, listeners can get confused: before they even know who's speaking or what it's about, they have to adjust to a new voice.

Build a bridge to take listeners into the clip
It's important for there to be a logical flow from cue to clip. The sentence before the bite must prepare the listener for what the speaker is about to say. Sometimes, a newsmaker's first sentence can be knocked off the clip, and used in the cue instead.

The cue should not repeat the clip
It sounds terrible if the story runs like this:
CUE: A family of four was found murdered in their home in Bloemfontein after

Format for a voicer that includes a clip

Stations have different styles for writing a script because they have different needs. This is one example of how a script could be written to make it as clear as possible what is going on. Notes explaining different features are in **bold italics – like this**.

Tooth **(slug or filename – should agree with the name of the file in the computer, the cart or MD)**

CUE: **(Cue material – read by presenter to introduce the report)**
Australia has asked South Africa to help chase a trawler suspected of poaching a rare fish species near the Antarctic. As Ace Tshabalala reports, an Australian fisheries patrol boat has been in hot pursuit of the trawler for over ten days already.

NARR: **(Body of voice report, read by reporter)**
The Uruguayan-flagged ship Viarsa was spotted around 4 000 kilometres south west of Australia more than a week ago. It ignored repeated radio orders to stop, and fled westwards with an Australian vessel giving chase. It is believed to have an illegal haul of Patagonian toothfish aboard, a sought-after delicacy that sells for some $24 per kilogramme. Australia has now asked for assistance from a South African Antarctic supply ship that is in the area. South African government official Horst Kleinschmidt says the trawler is dodging into an area of dangerous loose ice where its Australian pursuer can't follow. **(Last sentence introduces the speaker, and leads into the clip. It is sometimes called a throw.)**

CLIP: 17 secs **(Indicates length of clip)**
(Transcription of the clip) The Viarsa got into trouble yesterday, it got enclosed by ice, not pack ice, but it's trying to free itself from that. So its progress at the moment is impeded.

NARR: **(Reporter continues)**
Kleinschmidt says the South African ship is also hampered by the high winds of the icy Antarctic winter. He says South Africa is keen to help, since poachers of the Patagonian toothfish operate across the Southern oceans and are threatening the species. For Sandi FM, this is Ace Tshabalala in Johannesburg **(Standard Out Cue, SOQ, or signoff)**

DO IT!

1) Draw up a checklist of ten characteristics for good soundbites, following this pattern:
To earn a place on air, a soundbite should:
   a) Be easy to hear
   b) ...
   c) etc
2) Listen to a few bulletins on your favourite radio station, and one other station that you don't usually listen to. Write notes about how they sound. How much sound do they use? Do they use mainly telephone clips, or do they use other kinds too? Use the checklist you wrote under the previous question to evaluate their use of sound.
3) The following is the transcript of part of a statement made on June 14 2005 in Parliament by President Thabo Mbeki, releasing deputy president Jacob Zuma from his duties after a court finding that Zuma and his financial adviser, Shabir Shaik had a 'generally corrupt relationship'. Imagine you had this material on tape, and you are preparing for bulletins that afternoon. Which clip would you choose? Pick out two further clips that you could use in later bulletins. Each clip should be around 20 secs – probably no more than around 50 words. Write some notes motivating your decision.

Extract of Thabo Mbeki's speech:

Madame Speaker;
Having said all this, it remains for us to answer the question as to how we should respond to some of the issues raised in the judgment handed down by Justice Squires.
It seems self-evident that, arising out of the judgment in the Durban Trial, there will be continuing legal processes in the higher courts. These processes will have a bearing on normal enquiries that the law-enforcement agencies may wish to undertake and on [any] follow up that Parliament may embark on in relation to any of its Members.
I am fully conscious of the fact that the accused in the Schabir Schaik case [may] have given notice of their intention to lodge an appeal. I am equally aware that a superior court may overturn the judgment handed down by Justice Squires.
However, as President of the Republic I have come to the conclusion that the circumstances dictate that in the interests of the Honourable Deputy President, the government, our young democratic system, and our country, it would be best to release the Hon Jacob Zuma from his responsibilities as Deputy President of the Republic and Member of the Cabinet.
Necessarily, we will continue to monitor and respond to all developments in relation to this and other relevant legal processes.
Personally, I continue to hold the Hon Jacob Zuma in high regard, and I am convinced that this applies to most Members of Parliament. We have worked together under difficult and challenging conditions for thirty years. In this regard, I wish to thank him for the service that he has rendered as part of the Executive, at national and provincial levels, sparing neither strength nor effort to ensure that, with each passing day, we build a better life for all South Africans.
I am certain that I speak on behalf of all who have served with him in Cabinet when I say that we shall remain friends, colleagues and comrades in the service of the people. And, as government, we shall continue to draw on his experience and expertise where the need arises.
In due course, I shall announce the necessary changes in the Executive to take account of the void that the departure of Deputy President Jacob Zuma has created.
I thank the Honourable Members for their presence at this Joint Sitting of the Houses of Parliament and for the attention they paid to what we had to say to address a difficult situation.
I trust that what we have done today, and will do in future, together, will continue to strengthen our democracy, reinforce the accountability of those who hold public office, and deepen the confidence of the masses of our people in their elected representatives and our organs of state.
I thank you.

4) Imagine you have only the text version of the statement. Write a cue and a voice report based on the events in parliament, for use in the bulletins that afternoon. The report should be 40 secs long (give or take 5 secs) without the cue. Use the format outlined above. You may need to do some background research to be able to include enough context.

5) Listen to the interview with an Iraq war protester on the CD. Choose a clip, and write a cue and voice report that includes the clip.

an apparent robbery. The police say a team of top detectives are working night and day to track down the killers. Superintendent Chris Wilken.

WILKEN: We have a team of top detectives working night and day to track down the killers.

The BBC says: 'Repetition makes for rotten radio.'[2]

Introduce the speaker

The cue needs to say clearly who is about to speak. When introducing a reporter, most stations use a formula like 'Sipho Tshabalala reports', 'Sipho Tshabalala has the story' or the like. Don't use those phrases for newsmakers, they are not reporting the story like the station's own journalists do. And make sure that you clarify which voice will be heard first. It is confusing if you tell people they are about to hear Sipho Tshabalala, and they then hear the voice of an angry demonstrator.

Back announcements

Where you have used an unusually long piece of sound, or a voicer has been edited so as to lose the reporter's outcue, the newsreader may 'back announce' the speaker. This simply means identifying the speaker again afterwards: 'That was Ace Tshabalala reporting from Mdantsane'.

1 SABC Radio News. *The Journalist's Manual.* Johannesburg: published by author, undated. p7.
2 BBC, *The BBC News Styleguide,* 2003, posted at http://www.bbctraining.com/pdfs/newsstyleguide.pdf, accessed on 5 October 2005. 35

Chapter **7**

Controlled conversations: Interviewing

John Perlman, the anchor on SAfm's Morning Live programme, tells the story of an interview early on in his career that was not going well. Silvino Francisco, South Africa's top snooker player, was limiting his answers to two words each. 'Nothing verbose like four words, or six. Just two,' writes Perlman.[1]

But then he challenged Francisco: 'I must say, snooker doesn't look like a very demanding game. Half of the time you are sitting down, watching the other guy play.' Suddenly, says Perlman, 'the interview opened up, wide. 'Do you know what it feels like to sit there?' he asked, suddenly interested, definitely irritated. 'If you're 1-0 down in a soccer match you run like hell to get a goal back. If you

THE LEARNING CURVE

Tough Talking

Ace decided it was time to make a move. She had smiled at him, they'd been on a job together, they shared a desk. That was something, but not enough. He had kept his eyes and ears open for any indication that she had a boyfriend, but found nothing. The trick was to find the right moment, and to be masterful. Women liked that.

His chance came during lunchtime, when they were alone in the newsroom. He left the room, so that he could come back in and perch on the edge of their desk. 'Hey, babe,' he said. 'What about you and me going out Friday?

Lerato looked up and arched her eyebrows. 'Babe?' she repeated slowly. 'I think you're getting a bit ahead of yourself.' And she calmly went back to her work. Ace could have died.

He needed to get out of the office. On the spur of the moment, he asked Liz whether he could go down to the hospital, where three children were sick with typhoid, fighting for their lives. 'Maybe I can talk to their relatives.'

She looked at him doubtfully. 'Those kinds of interviews are quite tough to do. I suppose you could see what's going on there. Just keep your phone open, in case I need you back here. And don't forget that pause button.'

Ace looked down uncomfortably.

At the hospital, he found his way through the crowded outpatients department to the intensive care unit, which was much quieter. On a long wooden bench, a woman sat with her face in her hands. She did not move.

Ace sat down next to her. 'Ma,' he said gently. 'I'm so sorry. Is it your child in there?' She looked up, as if returning from a faraway place. 'My Sipho,' she said softly.

Ace steeled himself. 'I'm from the radio. Would it be possible to talk to you with my tape? People want to know about what happened.'

'They have been very good,' she said. He took that as a yes, and brought out the minidisk and mike. 'Tell me about Sipho,' he said.

She began telling him about her little boy, and then, with little prompting, moved on to how he had become ill, the dirty water in the streets, the smell. Ace felt her need to speak, to put everything together. 'What will I do? What will I do? He is my son.' She fell silent. He turned the machine off and sat for a while. 'Can I put this on the radio?' he asked, just to make sure. She looked directly at him: 'People must know.'

Back at the office, Liz listened to the interview. 'That's really good, Ace,' she told him. 'Give me a clip for the next bulletin. And then clean the interview up – it's a bit long, five minutes or so. But it's strong, I don't want to lose too much. We'll use it in Newsday.'

make one mistake in snooker you are gone. You sit there with plenty of time to think about that mistake, with between 16 and 20 million people watching you on TV, while the guy is murdering you. And there's nothing you can do about it. That's what's criminal about this game."

From then on, Francisco talked and talked, until the only way Perlman could end the interview was by simply getting into his car and driving off.

The interview is the basic tool of every reporter, and generates most of the information that finds its way into the news. Most interviews are straightforward affairs, but it takes skill to get the information you need. It takes even greater skill to lift an interview to a higher level where they reveal something substantial or surprising about their subject. In describing his encounter with the snooker champion, Perlman says he doesn't know whether it was 'irritation or inspiration' that caused him to ask his provocative question. Sometimes, luck can turn a difficult interview into a successful one – but it's better to rely on skill.

For the broadcaster, interviews have an even greater importance than for a print journalist. They need to deliver not only the information for writing up, but the sound of the speaker. There's an element of performance in the broadcast interview – technical quality, the source's personality, voice and delivery matter. At the same time, it 'is essentially a spontaneous event,' writes David McLeish. 'Any hint of its being rehearsed damages the interviewee's credibility to the extent of the listener believing the whole thing to be 'fixed'.'[3]

An interview is a controlled conversation. The interviewee is the star of the show. The interviewer's job is to get them to open up, tell their story, perhaps account for their actions. The interviewer's own opinions should not get in the way. Some interviewers have become celebrities, and they end up attracting attention in their own right. But in general, interviewers should stay out of the limelight.

They do have to remain in control. Valerie Geller writes: 'If the interview heads in a dull direction, grab it, and steer the discussion elsewhere ... Your audience will appreciate it if you can keep your guests away from intricate and technical answers.'[4] And, one might add, if you can prevent the guest from avoiding important questions.

Some people talk about interviewers adopting an informed but naïve attitude. That means they know a reasonable amount about the subject, but they are prepared to ask the questions ordinary people might have.

The attitude should be polite but professional. It's wrong to treat your guest arrogantly, as if you're doing them a favour, but it's also wrong to 'ask questions from your knees', as SABC presenter Freek Robinson says.[5] The interviewee is giving up time to speak to you, but you have a job to do, and you're doing it on behalf of the audience.

What's it for?

Radio journalists do interviews for different purposes, and this will affect the equipment you use and your approach. Some interviews may have more than one purpose.

No sound needed

You are just looking for some information to use in a story. This could involve a quick phone call and a single question, or it could involve a long discussion to get background on a story. But you don't need to record anything – all you need is a notebook and a pen, just like a newspaper reporter.

Interviewing for a soundbite

Under these circumstances, you need to record, either face-to-face or telephonically. But the interview is likely to be short – you're only going to be using around 20 seconds, so there's no point in doing a lengthy interview. However, you may need to ask several questions in your area of interest so that you get a good clip. Ideally, you will have enough material to run a few soundbites in different bulletins.

Prerecording an interview for broadcast

If you intend to broadcast the interview as a whole, it's important to pay attention to the structure. The questions need to follow logically one after the other. You will be able to edit out mistakes – both interviewer and interviewee can simply begin a sentence again if they feel they have made a mistake, or if there was a sudden background noise.

Live interview

Every word counts. There are no second chances. It should not be too long, and it needs to be managed carefully. More than with other interviews, listening is critical, otherwise you may miss an opportunity for an important follow-up question. Also, you may have to cut the interviewee off politely but firmly, jumping in with a new question if she pauses. For a three-minute interview, you are unlikely to have time for more than about four questions.

The question of editing

Material can be edited to make it clearer, cut out hesitations, noise or mistakes – although the speaker's meaning may never be distorted. But editing takes time, which is a scarce commodity in many radio newsrooms. It is a simple trade-off: if you do have time, you can polish your material; if speed is all-important, you'll have to live with some rough edges.

If you do intend to do some editing, you can ask the speaker to repeat him- or herself during the interview. The danger here is that he or she may get flustered the second time around, or may use phrases like 'as I said', which make the clip impossible to use. It is usually best to ask in a different way, as if you're trying to clarify the matter in your own mind.

Types of interview

Informational
The simplest kind of interview is where you want the interviewee to share information she has. You may be talking to a police spokesperson about a murder investigation, for instance, or to a municipal official about a new housing project.

Analytical
Interviews with commentators, observers and experts are very common. When the minister of finance presents the national budget, radio stations fall over themselves to get economists to discuss it. They are basically asking for analysis: what does this budget mean?

Probing
Journalists can use an interview to challenge public officials about an issue, to hold them to account. If a bus full of kids has crashed into a dam, the local radio may interview the relevant municipal official to find out why safety precautions were inadequate, and why the road wasn't blocked off from the dam. Alternatively, there may be a need to talk to the bus owner about the roadworthiness of the vehicle.

Interviews of this kind can become adversarial and hostile. It is reasonable to ask hard questions that the public wants answered, but it is important to remain professional and polite. The interview should not become a lynching. Some interviewers think they are being tough, when they are simply being rude.

Emotional
This is an attempt to explore somebody's feelings. You may, for instance, want to talk to the survivors of the above bus accident. These interviews are quite common, and need to be handled with sensitivity. Try to avoid the standard question: How do you feel (about the murder of your brother, eg.) What is he going to say? With a little thought, more original questions can be developed that may draw more interesting answers.

Vox pops
The term comes from the Latin for the 'voice of the people'. This is a device to get the opinions of ordinary people onto the radio. Journalists go out onto the street and ask people what they think of, say, the government ban on plastic bags, the price of petrol or something. It is important to try to get a mix of people, old and young, men and women, white and black. The responses are then cut together and played as a single item of two or three minutes. It can be used to introduce a discussion of the issue, for instance.

> For emotional interviews the rule is to tread carefully when your foot is on somebody's heart, and then only walk where you have been given the right of way. – Andrew Boyd[6]

Preparing the interview

Research

The interviewer must be well informed about the subject. There's nothing more embarrassing than being corrected by the interviewee about something really basic that you should have known. You can get background information from previously published material (in newspaper archives on the Internet, for instance); from other knowledgeable sources (friends or enemies of the interviewee), colleagues who have dealt with the issue, or the interviewee him or herself. The Australian Broadcasting Corporation adds: 'Make sure you have asked yourself the first question – 'Why is this issue pertinent NOW?' And be clear on the interviewee's investment in the issue.'[8]

Find the right person

Journalists like to talk to the person at the top – usually, the more senior a person is, the more authority they will have to speak on behalf of their organisation. But sometimes, a person lower down will have more detail about what's going on. Of course, organisations will often decide who will speak on their behalf, and then you don't have much choice. If possible, it is a good idea to try for new voices. Too often, it's the same 'dial-a-quote' people who end up being interviewed.

Preparatory discussion

It is useful to have a short chat with the interviewee before you begin, particularly for a live interview. It allows you to get a sense of the person you are dealing with, decide on an approach, and develop some rapport with him or her. You can also make sure both sides understand what the interview will be about, and what the terms are – which programme it is for, when it is to be broadcast etc. It is not a good idea to discuss the issue in detail before you begin – it will make the actual interview feel – and sound – like a mere repetition.

Interviewees often ask to be showed the questions beforehand. It is usually best to sketch in general terms what you want to cover, preferably verbally. Interviewees have a right to know beforehand what ground you intend to cover, particularly if a bit of background research would deliver a better interview. But you should make it clear that you may need to explore issues that come up – most people will understand that. You also want to avoid the interview sounding unnatural, which it may if people come with scripted answers. And you should avoid a situation where somebody tells you while you are on air that she won't answer this question because it wasn't on your list.

Planning the questions

Most radio interviews run to little more than four or five minutes – so it's a good idea to plan the best way of using the available time. You may want to ease into the subject, starting with an easy question to allow the interviewee to 'warm

> **Interviewer:** What do you intend to do about the fact that the shopping centre collapsed, and five people died, Mr Mayor?
>
> **Mayor:** I am hereby resigning from my job. We should not have passed those building plans. I believe in accountability, and the residents of this town deserve better. I'm going.
>
> **Interviewer:** The civic association says you should take responsibility for the problem. What are you going to do about it?

up'. On other occasions, it might be better to go straight to the heart of the issue. Either way, the questions need to flow smoothly on from each other. In planning them, you have to forecast how you think the conversation will flow. But prepared questions must never be a straitjacket. They are there to give you a sense of the direction you want to go in, but you must listen to the answers, and shape your actual questions according to what is actually said. There's nothing worse than an interviewer who sticks to questions even though the actual answers have made them irrelevant.

You should have prepared questions – but you may end up not using them at all.

Techniques for successful interviews

Questions need to be short and clear. They are not there for you to make a long speech, or to show off how much you know. You're simply pointing the interviewee in the direction you want them to go. It should be clear what you're asking. It's best to start questions with specific words like: Who? When? Where? What? Why? How much? How?

Wide or narrow questions

How much wiggle-room do you want to leave your interviewee? The narrowest of all questions are those to which the answer is either yes or no. These are sometimes called 'closed' questions, and they are only appropriate if you want to pin the interviewee down on something quite specific, and if you then move on to more 'open' questions that allow for discussion of whatever it is. In general, you should ask questions that allow the interviewee some room to say more than yes or no. But beware of making the questions too wide. A question like 'what about the power failures?' is so wide open that the interviewee can respond any way they like.

Double questions

Avoid asking two questions in one. The interviewee will usually choose the easier one to answer, and forget the other one, sometimes by mistake, sometimes intentionally. Ask one question at a time.

Statements

Don't make statements in the hope that your interviewee will respond. They may not, leaving you sounding silly.

Leading questions and accusations

Avoid questions that try to put the interviewee into the wrong by using emotional language. If you ask: 'Why did you fail in your constitutional duty to provide safe water to the town's poor people?' you're simply going to irritate the interviewee, and it adds nothing to the listener's understanding. Some journalists think tough questioning must be aggressive, but in fact listeners may end up siding with the interviewee who they feel is being 'victimised'.

Preventing evasion

But you must prevent the interviewee avoiding important questions. It is possible to do this while staying polite and professional. Politicians are very skilled at pushing the conversation into a direction that favours them, and a good interviewer will resist these tactics, if necessary by simply restating the question. If it is possible that the question has been misunderstood, put it in different words.

Body language

In normal conversations, people often signal they are listening by saying something like 'um', 'yes' or 'oh' from time to time. For a radio interview, verbal signals get in the way, and should be avoided. But you need to show the interviewee that you are paying attention. Keeping eye contact and nodding help show that you are interested. A tough question asked with a smile may be more easily answered. You may need to take some notes, but this should not disrupt the flow of the interview.

Ending

When you're done, thank the interviewee. If you're prerecording, check the person's title, name and preferred pronunciation. Make sure you have a contact number for future use – you may need to clarify something on this story, or you may need to talk to this person again for another one. Treat people professionally, and they will talk to you again. Before you leave, make sure the interview is actually on the tape.

CHECK IT OUT!

- John Perlman: The art of the interview. In: Adrian Hadland (ed). Changing the Fourth Estate: Essays on SA journalism. Cape Town: HSRC Press, 2005.
- Andrew Boyd. Broadcast journalism: techniques of radio and television news. Oxford: Focal Press, 2002. Ch 8 & 9
- Francois Nel. Writing for the media in Southern Africa. Cape Town: Oxford University Press, 2005. Ch 7
- The BBC's training department offers free online courses in interviewing at http://www.bbctraining.com/onlineCourse.asp?tID=2555&cat=2772. There is also a selection of really disastrous interviews you can listen to.

Tips for interviewing on a shoestring

If you don't have facilities or time to edit interviews, get used to treating even pre-recorded interviews as if they were live. Do the interview to length, and make every second count.

DO IT!

1) Listen to interviews by two different people on radio. Analyse them carefully. Do they work? What kinds of interviews are they? What kinds of questions are being used? Do the questions follow logically? Can you hear places where the interviewer seems to have deviated from planned questions to follow up something that was said?

2) Prepare five questions for each of the following situations:
   a. Residents of Mitchell's Plain are furious about a spate of child disappearances. You're interviewing the police spokesperson about the issue.
   b. You're interviewing the local leader of the municipal workers' union about the breakdown in wage talks, and the fact that the union is considering a strike.
   c. You're interviewing a university academic about the prospects for a settlement in the municipal dispute.

3) Powerplay interview:
   You need to do this exercise with a friend. One of you is the reporter, interviewing the other, who is the superintendent of a hospital, Dr Brett Isaacs, who stands accused of spending R360 000 on redecorating his private offices while the children's ward lacks beds and other facilities. A baby died in the ward, and the parents have claimed it was due to the lack of a drip. However, the hospital has denied this was the cause. Both players need to prepare for the interview, which should last no longer than five minutes. Both are fighting for control of the interview – the reporter wants to expose the facts, the other wants to make the situation look better. Do the interview in front of a small audience, if possible, and record it, too. Afterwards, discuss it: who came out on top, and why? Which techniques did the two sides use? Which questions were asked? Did they work? (idea adapted from Andrew Boyd: Broadcast journalism).

1 John Perlman, *The Art of the Interview.* In: Adrian Hadland (ed). *Changing the Fourth Estate: Essays on SA Journalism.* Cape Town: HSRC Press, 2005. p 93.
2 From BBC training module, *Interviews from Hell.* Accessed at http://www.bbctraining.com/modules/2604/jonathan.html, on 15 March 2006.
3 David McLeish. *Radio Production.* Oxford: Focal Press, 1998. p37.
4 Valerie Geller. *Creating Powerful Radio.* New York: M Street Publications, 1986. p 86
5 Quoted in Francois Nel. *Writing for the Media in Southern Africa.* Cape Town: Oxford University Press, 2005. p 149
6 Andrew Boyd, *Broadcast Journalism.* Oxford: Focal Press, 2002. p 105
7 Quoted in Boyd, op cit, pc112.
8 ABC. (undated). *SABC Radio Journalism Training Notes.*

A studio can get very full

Chapter **8**

Equipment 2: In the studio

Radio stations have studios for different purposes. Broadcast studios can be set up in various ways depending on how much money the station has and what their programming is like. Some stations have specialised music or drama recording studios, but most have an all-purpose production studio, where ad spots, news items, promos and other items can be put together.

It is very useful to have 'news booths', which are equipped with just the basic equipment to put together a news item. They don't need to be larger than a desk, and don't need much more than a PC, a mike and a telephone hybrid. Depending on what field recorders are in use, some also have a cassette player

THE LEARNING CURVE

Cutting Words

'Won't you cut a soundbite or two from this interview with the doctor who's looking after those children?' Liz asked Ace. 'Lerato did it last night on the show, she was standing in, and I'd like to use it in the bulletins.'

'Sure.' This was something he could do well. He'd spent many hours on the computer, exploring Adobe Audition. He would show everyone, particularly Lerato, that he wasn't just a kid.

He cut three clips, and wrote cue material for them all, making sure they all referred to 'in an interview with Sandi FM's Lerato Moagi'. They ran throughout the morning.

After lunch, Lerato arrived for her shift, and Ace looked around, expecting to get some credit. But she did not look pleased. She marched over to Liz's desk, and demanded to know what had happened with her interview. 'Let's listen to it,' Liz said.

The doctor's voice came again over the computer's speakers. 'Their condition is very serious. It looks very grave, but we are doing what we can.'

Lerato said: 'Let's find the original.' A few keystrokes, and the doctor's voice came again: 'Their condition is very serious. Typhoid is a very serious illness. It is very important to begin treatment in the early stages of the disease. Fortunately in this serious case they were brought in as soon as the first symptoms appeared. It looks very grave, but we are doing what we can, and we remain hopeful.'

They turned to Ace. 'It was too long,' he protested. 'And she kept saying 'serious', and giving medical technicalities. She's saying they are very sick. What's the problem?'

Liz said: 'The problem is that you turned a hopeful statement into a virtual death sentence. It wasn't what she meant. And how do you think those families feel?'

Lerato did not even look at him. 'Liz, please don't let kids play with my stuff.'

---

or MD machine. However, these inputs can simply be plugged straight into the computer, too.

A 'controller' (also known as a sound engineer or technical producer) is sometimes in charge of the technical aspects of broadcast. But increasingly, radio stations are installing 'self-op' studios, in which the presenter or journalist also operates all the equipment. These arrangements are cheaper for the station, but it is harder for the individual presenter to keep track of all the technical issues while concentrating on the content of the show. Nevertheless, it is increasingly important for radio journalists to learn at least the basics of studio operation. The current journalism qualification also requires students who want to specialise in radio to know their way around a studio.

Studio equipment

The mixing desk (studio desk, control panel or control board)
At the core of any studio, 'this is essentially a device for mixing together the

various programme sources to form the broadcast output', writes Robert McLeish.[1] Its sources include microphones, CD players, tape decks, MD player, computer, telephone and others. Each source, or input, is on its own channel, and a fader allows that source to be put on air when required.

The desk will also offer a 'prefade' function that allows the technician or journalist operating the desk to listen to a source before putting it on air. In addition, there will be communication circuits that allow the controller to communicate with studios or outside broadcasts.

There are facilities to allow the programme to be monitored via loudspeaker. It is best to monitor 'off air', since this will allow any problems that may arise in broadcast to be picked up. Set the volume of the monitor and then leave it alone, otherwise you will not hear problems with the levels.

Microphones
Some technical details about different kinds of microphones were given in the chapter 5. In the studio setting, though, they can be set up in various ways, depending on what kind of programming is being produced. A music station may have just one mike for the DJ, who may also be operating the desk. Another station may have several microphones at a separate table, where participants in a studio discussion can sit comfortably.

Reel-to-reel tape decks
Once upon a time, these were the studio's mainstay. Quarter inch magnetic tape on big reels were used to play items into the programme. They have almost disappeared.

MiniDisk player
The studio version of the journalist's field recorder has the same basic functions. It's just bigger.

Turntable
What the reel-to-reel tape deck is to speech, and particularly news, the turntable is to music. Previously, all music was played from vinyl records. They have virtually disappeared, and those turntables left in studios are sorry, abandoned things.

CD player
Music can be played off CD – exactly the same CDs that are used in home entertainment systems. They offer better sound quality than records, they are more durable and easier to store. The players give indications of 'time played' and 'time remaining'. The recording is digital, and individual tracks can be accessed precisely and quickly.

CDs are also often used to store jingles, which can then be quickly and easily played into the programme.

The computer

PCs are taking over more and more studio functions. They can be used for editing and for playback, can store vast amounts of music and allow fully automated programming. A PC can be told to play a certain set of items in a given order, including speech, music and advertising spots, and be left alone to do so. Computer systems also allow stations in a network to place their own programming into material they are sharing with others. So stations can insert local ads into the ad break of a national show, and all without the listener hearing any odd breaks.

The telephone hybrid

This allows phone callers to be put on air. It simply takes the sound coming down a telephone line and makes it available to the mixing desk and therefore the broadcast.

Using the studio

It is important to prepare properly for any studio production or recording session. You need to:

- Understand the different functions of various pieces of studio equipment;
- Decide which equipment will be needed and make sure it is in working order;
- Make backup plans in case equipment malfunctions;
- Power up the studio equipment as specified by the manufacturer (it is just as important to power down properly afterwards). Incorrect powering up can damage the equipment and be unsafe for operators. This could scuttle production plans and harm the station's image and finances;
- Equipment needs to be tested in time for the production to begin, to make sure it is ready and in working order;
- It is important to make sure that the fader routing is correct. In other words the right piece of equipment should be linked to the correct fader on the desk;
- The studio must be prepared in every respect for the production. This can include bringing in chairs for a studio discussion, making sure that surfaces are clean and tidy, ensuring that air conditioning is switched on etc;
- In doing these preparations, it is important to ensure that all safety, health and maintenance requirements are met.

For a successful radio production:

- Audio levels must be set according to production requirements, and must be monitored constantly
- The right audio sources must be chosen and mixed
- Back-up recording should be made
- The equipment should be left in good working order and ready for the next production. Any faults should be dealt with immediately or reported.
- Any administrative tasks – like filling in a log – must be seen to.

Editing

A recording may be edited for a number of reasons, all off which make it more effective on radio.

For length

Time is precious on radio. The show may have space for four minutes of interview on a particular subject. If the interview is prerecorded, and the person chats on for seven minutes, half of it will just have to go.

To remove poor quality material

This could include audio that is technically bad, repetitive or uninteresting.

To change the order

In an interview, you may come back to a question you forgot earlier. In editing, you can move the question and answer into a more logical place in the interview, to make it flow better.

To allow for creative treatment

We can mix together speech, music and wild sound to add atmosphere to a report.

Common editing faults[2]

- The edit point has noises like clicks, drop outs, or sudden changes in background noise.
- The material makes no editorial sense – its meaning is unclear.
- The timing is wrong – pauses are too long or too short, creating an unnatural rhythm in the person's speech.
- Breaths sound unnatural. If you don't pay attention to where the speaker breathes, you may cut breaths out or leave two next to each other. Both would sound unnatural and strange.
- There are problems with the level, or volume. We talk about 'clipping' when the peaks are too high, which means the sound is distorting. The waveform on a computer will look like the tops have been cut off. If the levels are too low, the audio can't be heard properly. Sudden changes in level from one voice to the next can be disorientating.
- The tone of the voice changes suddenly – a smiling voice changes to a serious tone

Different ways to edit

NOTE: It is easy to change the meaning of somebody's words in editing. It is possible to take out the word 'not', or to remove some sentences that introduce some nuance, as Ace found in The Learning Curve episode in this chapter. This is NEVER acceptable. Under no circumstances should the edited version distort what the speaker intended to say.

When journalists worked with reel-to-reel tape, they used to use a technique known as cut editing. This simply meant that they physically cut the tape with a razor blade to take out any unwanted material, and stuck the tape back together again with special tape. It is also known as destructive editing, because the original recording is destroyed in the process. Many journalists ended up looking desperately on the ground for a crucial piece of tape that they had cut by mistake!

Another technique is dub editing, which can be used with different kinds of equipment. This involves playing the desired piece of audio, and recording it onto a second machine in exactly the right place. So you would record your first link onto one cassette machine, and then record the clip you want off another, then record your second link and so on.

Minidisk and solid-state recorders offer some capacity for editing in the field. This involves inserting track marks at different points, and then erasing, copying or moving the tracks. These are limited and cumbersome options, but can be used in a pinch.

Using Adobe Audition (Cool Edit)

Editing on computer has become far and away the most common method of working in the modern radio studio. Almost any computer terminal can be used, as long as it has a sound card, enough memory and processing power.

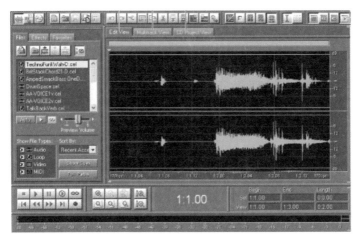

Adobe Audition showing a file in stereo

Adobe Audition in multitrack mode

There are several software packages available. In this section, we will look at some of the basic functions in Adobe Audition, which is one of the most popular programmes. It was previously known as Cool Edit. The programme functions of other well-known audio editing packages are not significantly different. A free audio editing programme called Audacity is available for download from http://audacity.sourceforge.net/.

This brief summary can only set out very roughly how the most important functions are tackled. To get really comfortable with the software, you need to practise on screen.

Recording

You can record audio from various sources into your PC, using Adobe Audition. The sound card in the computer will have various jacks, for input and output, and you need to plug your sound source – mike or field recorder, for instance – into the right jack.

You then need to make sure the record settings for the sound card are right. Click on the little loudspeaker at the bottom right hand corner of your screen. You will first see volume controls that look like a little mixing desk. To find the recording levels, go to options – properties – recording. This will allow you to make sure that the correct input is enabled.

If you now hit the record button on the transport controls (red dot, bottom left), Adobe Audition will create a new waveform (audio file). A dialogue box will ask you whether you want to work in mono or stereo, and what the sample rate and resolution should be. Ordinary settings for news purposes would be a sample rate of 32 000 or 44 100, mono and 16 bit.

Once you begin playing your source, you will be recording. Run the sound for a while first, to check the levels. The red bar on the bottom should peak at around − 3dB. Make adjustments by moving the relevant fader on the sound card's control panel. Once you're satisfied with the levels, record the sound for real.

A large box at the bottom of the screen indicates the time as the audio is recording (or playing). On the bottom right, there is another box that indicates time readings for whatever is in the window, and any piece you have selected.

Saving

Adobe Audition saves audio files like other Windows applications. Remember that the programme calls them 'waveforms'. You will find the save button under the file menu. You should give the file an easily recognisable name, and save it in the right subdirectory. Note that you will have the option of choosing a format for the file. The best one to use is mp3.

> **CHECK IT OUT!**
> - Robert McLeish, Radio Production. Oxford: Focal Press, 1998. Ch 2
> - The BBC's training division has an excellent set of online tutorials that will take you through the core aspects of digital editing, using Cool Edit Pro (now Adobe Audition). Find the tutorials at http://www.bbctraining.com/onlineCourses.asp.
> - The site itrainonline (www.itrainonline.org) contains a Multimedia Training Kit which includes modules on digital editing. Find it at http://www.itrainonine.org/itrainonline/mmtk/index.shtml.
> - Read the manual of any equipment you use, and use the help functions!

Playing

The transport controls in the bottom left hand corner look the same as on a stereo set or walkman. You can play, rewind, fast forward, pause, jump to the beginning or end. There is also a 'loop' button, which will play the track again and again. Normally, Adobe Audidion will play just the section on the screen, and then stop – but there is a button which will continue playing to the end. The space bar also acts as a play button.

The cursor appears as a yellow line, and will move along as the audio plays. You can position it by left clicking your mouse, if you want to listen from a particular point. (The left square bracket will mark a spot for later reference while it is playing.)

Zooming

A set of buttons just to the right of the transport controls allow you to zoom in on a section of audio. This is very useful for fine editing. You can zoom in or out, zoom into the beginning or end of a selected section or jump to a view of the whole piece of audio.

Scrolling

You can also scroll along the piece of audio by manipulating the green bar on the top, or the ruler underneath the display window. If you hold your cursor over either, it will turn into a little hand. By left clicking and holding it, you can drag the display to the left or the right.

Editing

You can cut and paste pieces of audio with the same functions used by other Windows applications. Define the piece you want to cut, for instance, by left clicking and dragging the mouse over the audio. You can make sure your selection is exact by zooming in, right clicking over the beginning or end and dragging it to the exact spot. Once you have made sure of your selection, you can cut it, or move it elsewhere. The application also has an undo button, so you can change your mind as often as you like.

Adjusting the levels

The levels of your final piece should be reasonably even – the peaks should be aligned. You can adjust the levels by going to amplitude, under the transform menu. Under the 'amplify' option, you can boost or reduce the levels of a section of audio or the whole file. You can use a slider to choose a percentage, where anything below 100% decreases the volume and anything above increases it. You can also choose from a number of presets, and you can fade in or out. You can also use the 'normalize' option, or create an 'envelope' to draw your own fade pattern.

Multitrack I: Inserting tracks

In the top left hand corner of the screen, there is an icon that takes you to the multitrack editor, where you can mix different sounds together. You can use the top track for your links, for instance, the next one down for ambient sound, and put the clips onto the next one down.

You can record directly into the multitrack editor, by enabling the record function on the track you want to use (click the red 'r' button on the far left) and recording in the normal way. You can also import audio files. You can 'insert' them one by one or you can open all the files you need at once by using the 'open' function under the 'file' menu. Under 'insert', you will find an option 'waveforms list' which will open a little box with all the open files. It's a good idea to reduce the box to a small size, and leave it out of the way in the bottom right hand corner of your screen. You can then drag and drop the files into position in the multi-track editor (left click and hold as you pull the file across.)

You can then also adjust the position of the file by right clicking, holding and dragging it along.

Audio formats:
Wav files save the audio in raw form, and are very large.
MP3 files are becoming the industry standard. They compress the data, and are therefore smaller, while keeping high quality.
RealAudio was one of the first audio formats and remains very popular. It is often used for streaming sound on the Internet.

Multitrack II: Playing

If you hit play, you will hear all the tracks playing simultaneously. If you want to pick out one or two tracks, then use the mute button (green 'm' on the far left of each track) to silence the ones you don't want to hear, or the 'solo' button (yellow 's' underneath the mute button) to play it alone.

Multitrack III: Editing

If you double click on any track, it will open in the single track editor and you will be able to cut, move or do anything else you need to.

Multitrack IV: Positioning tracks

The main aim of editing different tracks together is making sure they sound good together. You need to move the various tracks into the exact position where they need to be. You do this by right clicking on the track you want to move, and dragging it along. Then listen to the two together, to make sure you have the right spot. You can also use the cursor to mark a spot, and then move the track there.

Multitrack V: Levels

If two pieces of a voice need to be equalised, it is easiest to right click on the file to be adjusted, and choose the volume option. This gives you a little control panel, which you can adjust by entering a value at the top or using the slider. How do you know what to enter? Play the two tracks in turn, and work out the difference in peaks by watching the bar meter at the bottom of the screen.

Multitrack VI: Fading

The second crucial task in mixing a package is to make sure the levels of the different tracks are adjusted to each other. Background sound needs to be faded in or out, translations need to overlay the original etc. It is best to use 'envelopes' – which allow you to see and adjust levels at any point in the file.

Click the buttons 'show volume envelopes' and 'edit envelopes' on the top of the screen. This will display a green line at the top of every track. If you click anywhere on that line, you will create a 'node' that can be moved by left clicking on it and dragging it. You will need several nodes to create the right fade, so the background is audible, but does not get in the way of the link. Listen, and adjust the nodes, until you have the right fade. If you want to remove a node, just drag it right off the track.

Multitrack VII: Saving

It can take some time to mix a package, so it is essential to save your work regularly, so that you don't end up losing it.

Studios on a shoestring:

Any station needs a broadcasting studio, which costs a significant amount of money whatever you do. A station will need at least:

- two mikes and headphones,
- an eight channel mixing desk,
- a rack with minidisk, cassette and CD players,
- an amplifier and
- two speakers to monitor the output.

There are organisations which help community stations raise money for equipment. Contact the National Community Radio Forum for advice, at 011 403 4336 or ceo@ncrf.org.za. Their website is www.ncrf.org.za.

In the context of producing news, some field recorders provide limited possibilities to edit sound. But otherwise, the cheapest facility you need to edit sound is probably a computer. This could be used for editing soundbites, interviews and packages – as well as adverts and jingles. The PC needs a sound card, which will include input jacks so you can play recorded sound into it, and speakers so you can hear what you're doing.

Audacity is a free shareware programme for audio editing. You can download it from http://audacity.sourceforge.net/

DO IT!

1) Familiarise yourself thoroughly with the studio equipment you use.
2) Work through the BBC's online course on digital editing (http://www.bbctraining.com/onlineCourses.asp). If you do not have access to the Internet, make sure you familiarise yourself thoroughly with the editing software you are likely to use.
3) Edit one of the two long interviews on the CD down to 3 minutes (Either 'the rose has thorns' or 'train surfing'). Write a cue to introduce the interviews.
4) Record an interview on a newsworthy topic. You can also use the 'Powerplay Interview' that you conducted for Ch 5, Interviewing.
   a. Using digital editing techniques, edit the interview to a length of 3 minutes. If you do not have access to the necessary equipment, use whatever equipment you do have access to. You need to ensure that it includes both questions and answers, that it flows and makes sense, and that the technical quality is acceptable.
   b. Choose and cut three strong soundbites from the interview. They should be no longer than 30 secs each.
5) Record the voice report you wrote for exercise 5 in Ch 5, and insert the soundbite you chose for it.
6) A packaging exercise will follow the next chapter.

Multitrack VIII: Mixing down

Once you are happy with the whole piece, it has to be saved to a single waveform. Go to 'mix down' in the 'edit' menu, where you can choose whether the file should be stereo or mono. For news purposes, mono is usually better. The programme will mix all the tracks together, and you can then save the finished package in the usual way.

Note that once it is mixed, you won't be able to disentangle individual elements to adjust them. If you are uncertain about anything, you could keep the multi-track version (a 'session'), where you could make individual adjustments and then mix a new version.

Since audio files take up a lot of memory, it is a good idea to clear your computer of unwanted files once you have finished with them.

1 Robert McLeish, *Radio Production*. Oxford: Focal Press, 1998. p 15.
2 This list of faults is derived from ABC, *SABC Radio Journalism Training Handout 22*. unpublished, 1994.

Chapter **9**

Packaging:
A painting with sound

Longer radio reports that include the reporter's voice and other elements are known as packages, illustrated reports or features. In the context of news programming, they generally run for two minutes or more, usually between three and five minutes. When reports get significantly longer, they become documentaries.

Andrew Boyd writes: 'Packaging is useful for presenting a balanced account of two sides of an argument and for permitting the use of more elaborate production techniques to include sound effects or music. Unlike the standard interview, where the focus is on the interviewee, the package sets up the reporter as raconteur (storyteller) and guide.'[1]

THE LEARNING CURVE

Chicken and Egg

Lerato was pulling together the typhoid story for Friday's edition of Newsday, which always tried to wrap up the week's events. She was hard at work on the terminal, writing the script.

'So have you chosen your clips yet?' Ace asked.

'How can I choose the clips before I've got a script?'

Here was a chance to show her he knew a thing or two, thought Ace. 'But at tech they always told us to write around the sound. You have to choose strong bites, and then structure the story around them.'

Lerato was getting irritated. She didn't have time for this. 'Rubbish. You have to be clear on what you want to say. You can't just roam around with the story.'

'But sound comes first.' Ace was getting cross, and loud. Stupid woman! 'They all say that.'

'And that's your argument?' said Lerato in that superior way she had.

Liz glanced up. 'Come on, you two. You're both wrong, you know. You have to do both more or less at the same time.'

They both looked at her.

'You have to know what you want to say, and know what good sound you have. Then you make a plan, which covers sound and script. Then you write the script. You have to make sure that the two work together; you can't make either of them dominant.'

They are mainly found in current affairs programmes, as vehicles for pulling together a story that has seen several new developments over the course of the day. They can be focused very specifically on a hard news story, or look at a broader issue like land reform or be used for an obituary – complete with sound of the person, friends and enemies.

Packages are rare in South Africa. They can sometimes be heard on SABC stations, but even there sound is rarely used to its full potential. Other stations find they take too much time, effort – and therefore money. Some stations like Talk Radio 702 use mini-packages in news bulletins – where a few very short sound clips are inserted into the reporter's voicer, and the whole still remains within the usual time limit for bulletin items.

Which elements go into a package?

A cue

The package needs to be introduced by the presenter of the programme, just like a voice report or an interview.

Narration

The reporter guides the listener through the story on the basis of a script, which identifies who is speaking in the various clips and links them together. Some stations refer to 'links' or 'tracks'.

Clips

The package uses short soundbites from several speakers.

Ambient sound

A good package will also use relevant sound recorded on location: children playing, the sound of tractors, the chanting of demonstrators. In the context of news, the sound must be genuine. You can't go into a collection of fx, and use the sound of gunfire to illustrate a story about a robbery. That would make people believe that the sound came from the event you are reporting on, which it did not.

Music

Relevant music can help to create a mood. In the context of news, music would usually only be used where it is integral to the story, like in a report about a new kwaito star.

Fly-on-the-wall

A recording of people going about their business can take the listener to the scene of the action, and provide a powerful element of a package. In a story about educational reform, you could record a section of a science lesson at a local school, for instance: the children clattering with equipment, asking questions, the teacher answering. It is important to use sound that will 'make sense' to the listener – otherwise it adds little of value. Vague, unspecific sound is just noise.

Description

Remember that radio creates images in the mind of the listener. Some description written into the narration can help to bring a story alive. For instance, if you're using the science lesson mentioned above, you could devote a few sentences to describing the scene: broken windows, perhaps, the shining faces of keen kids, posters on the walls or the like. You can only do this properly if you observe carefully while gathering your material. You need to keep notes on what you see, so that you can build it into the script later. Make sure you get it right: if you report that the teacher wore a t-shirt saying '100% Zuma – innocent until proven guilty', you'd better be sure those were the exact words.

Silence

A package is unlikely to use long stretches of nothing at all. But sound needs to be properly spaced, it needs to breathe. A pause in the middle of a clip can say a lot about the speaker's state of mind.

A plan of action

Slapping together a minute and a half on today's court appearance for the afternoon show, with sound of the prosecutor and of the defence lawyer, doesn't take much time. And it shouldn't: in that context speed matters more than production values. But as soon as you get more ambitious in length, use of sound and scope of the report, the process can become more complicated. It's good to have a clear plan of action.

Plan your project

Even before you begin gathering material, it's a good idea to develop a clear idea of what you want to do. The key questions are:

• What is the story going to be about? This is not as easy as it may sound. A lot of journalism falls flat on its face because the reporter has only a woolly idea of what the focus is. It is useful to write a short statement, defining the aim. Usually, you will need to sell the idea to the news editor, particularly if it's going to take time and resources. That can be a difficult, but useful process, in which you are forced to explain and defend the idea.

• Who do I need to talk to? List the sources your focus requires. If it's about a shortage of science facilities in the schools of a particular area, there's little point in talking to an English teacher – you see how important a clear focus is?

• What opportunities are there for sound? You need to plan for sound, and set out to get sound that will enrich the report.

Gather the material

You need to remain flexible. Some sources are going to be unavailable, and new information may arise which forces you into a different direction. How much do you need? It depends on your timeframe: the more material you have, the more choices you have about what to use – but the more time it will take to process everything.

Log or transcribe the material

When you've got everything together, you need to develop an overview of everything you've got. Some people log their material – they make a list of it, indicating where it is to be found. Others transcribe it roughly. In both cases, it's important to create a 'directory' so that you can find the material you need quickly. If you are using a minidisk, break the interviews into shorter tracks so that you can scroll through them quickly,

> ### CHECK IT OUT!
> • McLeish, Robert, Radio Production. Oxford: Focal Press, 1998. Ch 20.
> • Developing Radio Skills, an online course developed by Fiona Lloyd for the International Women's Media Fellowship is at http://iwmf.org/training/radio/index.php
> • How to produce a doc, by Dmae Roberts, is a detailed guide to putting together a radio documentary. It's to be found at http://www.stories1st.org/words.php
> • Canadian Broadcasting Corporation's programme Dispatches carries many sound-rich features. You can listen to some at http://www.cbc.ca/dispatches/
> • National Public Radio in the US airs 'Radio diaries' – documentaries put together on the basis of sound that ordinary people have collected over long time periods, up to two years. You can listen to some at http://www.radiodiaries.org/

and indicate on your log or transcript where the material is. If you're using a cassette recorder, use the timer to keep track.

It takes time at this stage, but saves time later while you are scripting and packaging. It can be enormously time-consuming to search for a particular clip somewhere in a long interview.

In the process of logging, you will also identify the strong clips.

Make a rough plan
Now you need to plan your package, deciding more or less how it will flow, and which clips you will be using.

Write the script
The detail needs to be worked on next. You need to write the links, taking care to integrate the sound well. Speakers need to be properly introduced, ambient sound must be supported by the narration if necessary, the ideas need to flow logically. To do this properly, you will need the exact words of the clips you want to use. You will need to listen to the clip, and at this stage it is useful to transcribe the words exactly, so that you can judge whether your words and the clip or wild sound work together, whether the clip is clear enough and whether any editing will in fact work (the words are not spoken so quickly that they can't be cut, for instance). If you note the length of the clip, you will be able to make a rough estimate of the length of the piece before packaging – if you've been given a maximum of 4 minutes, and your material runs to 8, it would be better to cut it back at this stage.

Have the script edited
Somebody else needs to look at the script to give you feedback. A second pair of eyes often picks up problems you have missed. This can be done just on the basis of the script, as long as you have transcribed the clips. Otherwise, your editor may need to listen to the clips, which will take more time.

Record and package
At this point, you go into the studio to put the whole thing together. You'll need to record your narration, dub the sound you want to use and mix the whole item together. You may need to make some adjustments at this stage, for length, clarity or other reasons.

If you have rushed earlier stages of the process, this last stage may take a very long time. A huge amount of studio time is wasted when people go

Tips for producing packages on a shoestring
It is possible to produce a package with a single recorder, and without doing any work in the studio: you record every element of the feature in exactly the right order onto your recorder, and to exactly the right length. This requires careful research and planning. If you can't cut anything out, you will have to make sure that every bit of sound is right. You use the pause button between different elements: while you prepare your own linking words, or move to the next interview. You can even use ambient sound, by recording a brief piece of location sound before you begin an interview.

Idea drawn from John van Zyl (ed), Community radio: the people's voice. Johannesburg: Sharp Sharp Media, 2003 , pp 76 – 79.

into the studio with a vague idea of what they want to do – they always end up searching and searching for that clip they just know was there, but can't find. If you have done everything thoroughly, the actual packaging need not take very long.

DO IT!
- Listen to some packaged reports on the website of the CBC's Dispatches programme, given in the Check it out! box above. Take careful note of how they use different kinds of sound.
- Listen to packaged reports on one of SAfm's current affairs programmes (AM Live, Midday Live, or PM Live), or another station. Take careful note of how they use sound.
- Produce your own package, on a subject of your choice. It needs to include the voices of at least three different sources, and some ambient sound, and should run to at least three minutes. Make sure you follow the plan of action outlined above, including making a clear plan; logging and writing a proper script. Follow the script format given below.

Format for a package script

(notes in brackets)

Dibs **(slug or filename)**

CUE: **(Cue material – read by presenter to introduce the report:)**
Nelson Mandela turned 85 years on Friday, and South Africa is wall-to-wall with events, tributes and celebrations. As Ace Tshabalala reports, every conceivable person and organisation is getting in on the act – and many companies see real benefit in expressing good wishes.

NARR: **(Report begins with reporter's voice)**
Back in 1964, Nelson Mandela was facing a death sentence for treason.

CLIP: MD AA, track 12. 15 secs **(indicates where clip is to be found, in this case on minidisk AA, track 12. This helps in production, whether you're putting the piece together yourself or somebody else is. Also indicates length of clip, so producers can calculate overall length)**
01:27 **(Indicates the beginning of the clip on the MD)** I have fought against white domination, and I have fought against black domination. It is an ideal I have lived for, but it is an ideal for which I'm prepared to die. 01:42 **(Indicates the end of the clip on the MD) (Text of clip)**

NARR:
After serving 27 years in jail, becoming South Africa's first democratically elected President and an international icon and then retiring, he's now turned 85. It's a very different country that is celebrating the day.

CLIPS: MD B, track 2. 22 secs
00:12 (Song): father of our nation, we praise and love you, ... Mandela..
(radio presenter): A song dedicated to the birthday boy, the birthday granddad, the birthday man
(Phone message): (ring, ring), Thank you for calling and being part of this wonderful birthday celebration. Please start recording your message after the tone. (beep)

NARR:
In a tent outside his Johannesburg home, Mandela greets a group of some 20 disabled children who have come to wish him happy birthday.

CLIP: MD B, track 3. 7 secs in clear
7:22 Hello how are you?
Fade under: **(instruction to producer to fade clip under the narration to follow)**

NARR:
85 birthday cakes have been built into a tower by military chefs. On a table, another three cakes are arranged. Sean Crystal, a manager at a hotel chain, says his company has sponsored the cakes.

CLIP: MD B, track 9. 8 secs
00:03 We are quite honoured to present Mr Mandela with these three cakes, sponsored by Southern Sun. 00:11

NARR:
One of the cakes bears the logo of national carrier South African Airways. The company's chief executive Andre Viljoen is on hand to tell Mandela that the first of a new fleet of planes is to be named in his honour. He's quite upfront about the benefits the company gets from being associated with the world-famous statesman.

CLIP: MD B, track 10. 23 secs
1:30 we're a world-class brand now, (CUT: we've been around for many years now, there are many other airlines, that aspire to our levels of service, ENDS CUT) **(instruction to do an internal edit in clip)** and having a man of this stature as our patron is for us a great honour. 1:53

NARR: The name Mandela has enormous power, and it's jealously guarded. His organisation has taken the precaution of copyrighting it, and permission to use it is rarely given. But when it comes to an event like the 85th birthday, it's open season. The media are full of advertisements in which copywriters use their best skills to build a connection between the company's brand, the birthday and the brand Mandela.

CLIP: MD B, track 5
cheers, plane noise
fade up sound under:

NARR:
Back at the birthday tent, South African Airways' newly named aircraft, the Nelson Mandela, thunders low overhead, as the man himself waves and onlookers cheer.

CLIP:
Bring up clip briefly into clear, then dip under:

SOQ:
For Newsday, this is Ace Tshabalala in Johannesburg

1 Andrew Boyd, *Broadcast Journalism: Techniques for Radio and Television News*. Oxford: Focal Press, 2002. p 245.

A newsreader concentrates on her script

Chapter **10**

Around the world in three minutes: The bulletin

'Give us 22 minutes, we'll give you the world.' – slogan of Westinghouse All News Radio[1]

The 24-hour news format sees stations broadcast nothing but news, updating and repeating constantly. They assume that people will tune in only for one segment of around 20 minutes, and then go elsewhere. No station in SA has yet tried this approach.

Radio bulletins are the sprinters among news outlets. While TV is still struggling with lights and print is writing headlines, the radio bulletin has broadcast the news, followed up several angles, dealt with reaction and moved on to the next story.

Radio stations squeeze the latest news into a few minutes at the top of every hour. Bulletins don't take up much time, and their regularity

THE LEARNING CURVE

Up to the Minute

The one o'clock bulletin was just ten minutes away when the phone rang. Ace was alone in the office with Jack, who was putting the finishing touches to the running order. He was leading with a story that had been running all morning: a busload of German travel agents who were being shown the delights of Cape Town had been robbed in Khayelitsha. It was a bit far for Sandi's listeners, but it was the strongest he had.

Ace picked up the phone. 'This is Dr Moodley from the hospital,' said a voice. 'I thought you might like to know that we have just had six more admissions of children from Luanda camp. They also seem to have typhoid.'

'Could I record a few sentences on that?' said Ace. 'I just need to transfer the call.'

He covered the mouthpiece with his hands and told Jack what the doctor had said. Jack was immediately interested: 'Let's try to get it into one o'clock. It's a strong lead. You record the clip.'

It seemed hardly enough time, but Ace was going to do his best. He recorded the doctor, thanked her and called up the file on the screen. He needed 20 seconds.

'I need that clip,' shouted Jack. 'Tell me what she said, so I can write the cue.'

Trying to recount the basics of the story and listen to what he had on the screen, Ace could think only of the time. He did not dare even glance at the clock. Where were the 20 seconds he needed? It was all strong.

'No time left,' said Jack and leapt up. 'I'll just run it hard, I've got enough for that. We'll use the clip at two.' He was out of the door.

When he returned a few moments later, Ace began to apologise. But Jack cut him short with a smile. 'Don't worry. There really was very little time. You'll get faster. At least we had the story.'

provides the listener with a sense of security that they haven't missed anything of importance. During drive-time, headlines at the bottom of the hour may be extended to become another bulletin.

Some stations have experimented with placing the bulletins at other times of the hour – every 20 minutes, for instance. But most bulletins remain at the top of the hour. When really momentous things happen, a station may carry a newsflash, where normal programming is interrupted for a report that can't even wait for the next bulletin.

Compiling a good bulletin takes a lot of skill. The pressure is substantial: the moment one bulletin is completed, work must begin on the next one.

On the one hand, the compiler must get the stories for the next bulletin written and edited as quickly as possible, so that the reader has enough time to prepare to read it. At the same time, there needs to be enough flexibility to accommodate late-breaking news. After all, radio's advantage is speed. It would be a pity not to make space for important stories that come through in the minutes before the bulletin – or even after the bulletin has gone on air.

The headlong rush for the next bulletin might break down into these steps:

7:00 – 7:05:	Bulletin
7:05 – 7:20	Compiler checks through news sources for updates and new stories, makes provisional selection of items for next bulletin.
7:20 – 7:50	Compiler rewrites stories to be repeated, edits new items, chooses sound and finalises a running order. Around seven or eight items will be needed.
7:50 – 7:58	Newsreader gets the bulletin to go through, while compiler checks for any important late stories.
7:58	Reader is ready to go to air.
8:00 – 8:05	Bulletin

The pattern will vary from station to station – if the newsroom is far from the broadcast studio, for instance, deadlines are likely to shift earlier so that the bulletin can be taken there. And on some days, everything happens all at once.

Choices

The bulletin should lead with the strongest, most recent stories available, and should include a balance of different kinds of items. The nature of that balance will vary between different stations, who will determine it according to the interests of their listeners.

Local or international?

One issue that always comes up is what the right proportion of local, national and international stories is. It is definitely wrong to develop an inflexible rule about this: there will always be stories that defy the pattern. When terrorists flew two airliners into the Twin Towers in New York, even stations with a strong focus on local news could not have ignored the story.

In general, audiences are much more interested in stories that happen close by. Andrew Boyd asks the rhetorical question: 'Is this story about me, about things happening on my doorstep, or is it about strangers 2000 miles away who I never knew existed?'[2] Community radio has a particularly strong mandate to focus on things happening locally. But stations should not rely on their audiences getting national and international news elsewhere – it's important to give listeners a full picture of their world. Disregarding everything that's not local can leave people cut off from important news.

For the individual bulletin compiler, this will be a matter of station policy. He or she may get a document setting out proportions of local, national and international items, but it's more likely that the policy will quickly become a matter of simple habit. He or she will 'just know' when a national story is big enough to include in a bulletin.

Not just politics
A bulletin should also be balanced in terms of the subject areas included. Politics, particularly, can easily dominate the news. It is important to include stories from other areas of life. Stories with a human angle are always worth considering.

Areas like sport and economics often have their own slots – sometimes outside the bulletins, sometimes a guaranteed segment in particular bulletins.

Sound
Soundbites and voicers liven up a bulletin, and contribute to its authority.

And finally
The last item in a bulletin has particular importance – it's the thing that is most likely to stay with listeners. Many stations like to give that slot to a light item, looking for a report that will leave listeners with a smile on their faces.

Transitions

It is important for the bulletin to read as a unified whole, the items following smoothly on from each other. Newsreaders should read through the whole bulletin before going on air – preferably aloud. Sometimes problems will only become visible when you look at the transition from one item to the next.

Signalling a new story
A short pause is usually enough to indicate the start of a new story.

Geography
The location of a story can be used to signal a shift, starting a new story with 'In Cape Town', 'Still in Germany' or 'Back at home', for instance.

Repetition of names
Be careful not to repeat names of people or organisations unnecessarily. For instance, if you've just had a story about the Minister of Foreign Affairs, Nkosazana Dlamini-Zuma, and the next one deals with her, too, try to link the two. It sounds silly to start the second story with her full name again: it's easier to say something like: 'The minister also ...' or 'Dlamini-Zuma addressed'. If her name only occurred at the very beginning of the previous story, though, it's fine to repeat it in full. As always, the test is simple: does it sound clear and elegant?

Bulletins in series

One of the great challenges of bulletin compilation is to cater for two very different audience segments: those people who stay tuned for a long time, hearing

CHECK IT OUT!
- Valerie Geller. Creating powerful radio: a communicator's handbook. New York: M Street, 1996. Ch 14.
- John Zyl. Community radio: The people's voice. Johannesburg: Sharp Sharp Media., 2003. Ch 4.

bulletin after bulletin, and those who have just joined the station, and for whom the present bulletin is the first one for several hours, perhaps even of the day. The first group doesn't want the same old stuff that they have already heard; the second wants to be sure that the bulletin includes all the major stories they have missed.

Some radio stations have listeners who belong mainly to the first group: often younger people with busy lifestyles, who may stay with the station for no more than 20 minutes on average. Others have a listenership who turn the radio on in the morning and leave it on for the rest of the day. The movement of listeners in and out is likely to be greater during morning and evening drivetimes than at other times. But the solution to the problem is not to work out who is in the majority and cater for them. Stations need to appeal to both kinds, as far as possible.

Dropping order

They do this by ensuring that important stories don't disappear from the bulletins too quickly. If the President fires his deputy, it doesn't make sense to run the story once and then lose it. It's too important to risk some people who may have missed the bulletin not hearing about it.

Capital Radio, an independent station that used to broadcast from the Wild Coast of the Transkei, used to have a rule setting out how quickly a story could be dropped down the bulletin.

Bulletin 1	Bulletin 2	Bulletin 3
Story A: Leads	moves to place 2 or 3	drops further down
Story B: in place 2 or 3	drops further down	drops out
Story C: in lower place	drops out	

Of course, very strong stories would override this preference. In any event, it's wrong to be too rigid.

Keeping them fresh

The 'long listeners' are kept satisfied by ensuring that every bulletin sounds fresh, even if it contains some of the same stories as a previous bulletin. Some of this work needs to be done on the bulletin desk, but the reporter has much greater scope to develop different versions of a story because he or she has access to more information.

US radio trainer Valier Geller calls this 'multi-version' reporting. 'The multi-version method gives a story variety. It breaks the story up into pieces to keep people listening longer ... If the listener hears only one version of your report, he or she should feel 'satisfied,' but if listeners hear all of the parts, they should feel 'full.'"[3]

Reporters should be thinking of possibilities for different versions while reporting the story: the bigger the story is, the more versions will be needed.

A new development
The strongest way of keeping a story fresh is if there is a genuine new development in the story. A family is found murdered in their home; a few hours later, the police make an arrest. It's easy to keep the story fresh under such circumstances.

Generating a new angle
The radio station can find a new angle on a story by simply talking to roleplayers. With a family murder story, a reporter may get some fresh material from the police, neighbours, friends, family members or other people, even if there is no major development in the murder investigation. Analysts fill many holes in this way: you can always find some talking head to comment on a news event. In fact, analysts are heavily overused. It's not the most original way of keeping a story fresh, but there are stories that benefit from this kind of treatment.

Finding alternative angles in the material
Since bulletin reports are so short, there is usually enough material to write several versions. The family murder could be run on the basis of the murder itself ('A family has been found murdered ...'), the police investigation getting underway ('Police have drafted in every available officer to probe the murder of the Smit family ...'), the fate of a surviving child ('The 9-year-old son of the Smit family has been taken into care by an aunt. His parents were found murdered this morning.') or others. The reporter should write – and probably voice – each of these separately for use in successive bulletins until there is a new development in the story. The bulletin compiler can also reangle a story if she or he has the necessary material.

Vary the sound
A new clip can do wonders to freshen a story. Reporters should note usable soundbites as they record, noting where they are on the tape to save time later. Different versions can be built around each one. Lee Harris, a morning anchor at a New

Tips for putting together bulletins on a shoestring
Don't lift stories: Many community stations simply take stories from the local newspaper, or off a website, and use them. It is always better to generate your own stories, dealing with local issues. (If you have a subscription to a news agency like Sapa it is slightly different, since you are paying for the right to use the material.) If you do use stories published elsewhere, you should at least indicate where they come from.

Cut sound from a studio interview: A newsmaker comes into the studio and is interviewed live on an interesting topic: you should easily be able to get a couple of clips to use in the bulletins from the interview.

DO IT!

1) Listen to three bulletins that follow each other on your favourite radio station. Keep a note of the stories in each one, and how they have (or have not) changed between bulletins. Look at how the running order has changed from one bulletin to the next. Do you agree with their handling of the stories, or would you have done something differently?
2) The following story was used on your station early this morning.
   a. Suggest three sources that you could interview in order to get fresh material to update the story.
   b. Rewrite the story for later use, on the assumption that you have no new information

Residents of Mdantsane's Zone 9 are still in the dark this morning after a power failure that began around 7pm yesterday – just as many people were cooking supper. A spokesperson for the city council says there was a short circuit in a substation, which caused a fire. A team of technicians is this morning still working to restore power. The spokesperson says the technicians began work late last night. But residents are furious. Jimmy Baqwa of the civic association told Sandi FM that many people could not cook, and that children could not do their homework without power. He said there were too many power failures, and the city council should sort out the problem. This is the fourth time this month that there has been a power failure in Mdantsane. Municipal authorities have said the infrastructure is getting old, and needs to be replaced.

York station, says: 'Here's how you can crank out three or four versions of the same simple news story in a hurry: Use a lead-in, then an actuality. In the next story, paraphrase that actuality, then use a new actuality. Work your way through your best tape in this fashion, creating as many versions as you need, or until the story changes.'[4]

Reword the story
No story should run in exactly the same form in successive bulletins. At the very least, the bulletin compiler should reword the beginning of the story. See whether you can tighten or improve the writing, or simply vary the approach.

1 Quoted in Andrew Boyd, *Broadcast Journalism*. Oxford: Focal Press, 2002. p 126
2 Ibid, p141
3 Valerie Geller, *Creating Powerful Radio: A Communicator's Handbook*. New York: M Street, 1996. pp 136 - 137.
4 Quoted in Geller, op cit, p 138.

A production team gets
ready for broadcast

Chapter 11

A bigger canvas:
The current affairs show

A good current affairs programme – also known as a news show – can cover a lot
of ground. In the space of an hour or so, the show can give listeners an overview
of the latest news, explain and probe what it means, offer essential information
about traffic conditions or weather prospects, touch their hearts and give them
food for thought. Where the bulletins often have to sacrifice depth for speed,
these shows give radio journalists the opportunity to tackle subjects in depth.
There's simply more time to prepare, and more time on air.

   Current affairs shows are usually scheduled for drivetime, when people are
on the move and available to listen. The morning slot is particularly good for

THE LEARNING CURVE

One Story, Many Takes

Lerato was again presenting the evening show. Liz was producing, and she said to Ace: "We're going to have to tackle the story about these new typhoid cases in a big way, and I'll need you to help. OK?" And turning to the others, she added: "Let's talk about what needs doing."

Thatho was working on a feature about speed traps. "That will have to wait," said Liz. "I need you to find the families of these kids and talk to them. At the same time, let's get some vox pops from residents."

Lerato said: "We need to take a close look at sanitation in town."

"Your story, hey," said Liz. "It would make a good package for early next week, but I don't think we have time this afternoon. We need to set up Dr Moodley, the municipality – what else?"

Ace said: "What about province? They should have something to say."

"Good idea. Can you get onto it? And can you go back to the doctor, too? We need her live or pre-recorded. Let's go, everyone."

There was little time. Ace battled to get through to the provincial MEC for health. He phoned and phoned, leaving messages, trying to explain the urgency to all kinds of people in the MEC's office. Dr Moodley, by contrast, was easy: in fact, she agreed to come into the studio. "I'm happy to talk about this. It is an outrage that children are getting typhoid in this day and age," she told Ace.

It was almost time for the show to begin, when Thatho rushed back in. "Can somebody help edit this interview with one of the fathers? I'll put the vox pops together."

Liz said: "I'll do it. I think we have the doctor after the bulletin, go with the father in the second quarter hour, I've lined up the mayor after half past. We can make him listen to the vox pops. If the MEC comes back to us in time, we'll just squeeze him in. It looks like we won't have space for much else."

The show got underway, and Lerato was her usual assured, friendly self. She really was good on air, thought Ace. He could have listened to her for hours.

The mayor was not enjoying Lerato nearly so much, that was clear. He sounded very uncomfortable as she pressed him politely but firmly on why there was no clean water in Luanda, and why there was still a bucket system.

She made him listen to the vox pops: angry voices of residents, describing the stench and talking about how the buckets were sometimes not collected for ten days or more.

"What do you have to say to these people?" she asked.

Just then the phone rang. It was the MEC.

Liz put him on immediately after the mayor. He was outraged, concerned for the children, and promised to take action: "Sanitation is a basic right. I will personally make sure that the municipality sorts out this problem. It is their responsibility to deliver, to serve the needs of the people who elected them."

"The mayor really is taking the heat. Why don't we get him back quickly to respond?" Ace suggested.

Liz nodded.

Moments later, the mayor was back on air. This time, he sounded angry. "I heard the MEC's comments. It was not my intention to make these issues public, but he leaves me no choice. The public should know that we submitted plans for installing a proper sewerage system in Luanda. Those plans went to province eight months ago. We are still waiting for approval."

And with that the show was over. Lerato came out of the on-air studio, and smiled at Liz.

One Story, Many Takes, cont.
"Great show. It was fantastic to get the mayor back. He was furious! These guys are just passing the buck backwards and forwards. We'll have to follow up on this issue tomorrow."
Liz said: *"It was Ace's idea. He also got the MEC in the first place. That was well done."*
They were all smiling at him. But there was just one smile that really mattered.

current affairs. Valerie Geller writes: 'It starts the day, commands the highest ad rates, and requires the most up to date information so the listener can get out the door and face the day. A solid morning show can set the foundation for a solid radio station.'[1]

Morning news shows are difficult to organise: producers and presenters have to get up very early in the morning. They prepare the show while many others – including news sources – are still asleep.

But the editorial advantages are great. Morning shows are first out of the blocks – they can look at what was on TV the evening before, what is in the morning papers and what has come in from the wire agencies overnight and craft a show that is as fresh as a glass of orange juice. They can reflect overnight developments, and also look forward to the events that will mark the day, like a major court appearance or an expected government announcement. Listeners want this kind of service, as well as the weather, traffic conditions and other practical information they need right then.

And radio does all this while allowing listeners to get on with their lives. It is no wonder that radio rules the morning. It consistently attracts its biggest audience at this time of the day.

The evening drive usually brings a smaller peak, as people make their way home, cook, bath their children and the like. Shows at this time generally look backward, summarising the day's events.

The third popular time for current affairs shows is lunchtime. Available audiences at this time are smaller than at morning and evening drivetime. But there are still people on the move, or on a lunchbreak that allows them to listen to the radio, or in the kitchen preparing lunch.

Of course, there are significant differences between audience segments: for young people, afternoons are often good listening times, because they are at school beforehand.

Good current affairs programming does not happen by accident. It takes time, thought and preparation. Some stations are satisfied with a programme in which the presenter just sits behind the mike and chats about what's in the day's newspaper – and many don't have the resources to do much more. This chapter will look at ways of getting more out of the format, for the benefit of listeners and journalists. It's much more interesting for both.

Creating a programme

It's a strange truth that listeners want to be surprised, but also want a programme to be consistent. In fact, it holds true for all audiences. Newspaper readers, too, want to know that they will find particular kinds of features in the same place every day; they want the paper to feel comfortable and familiar in tone, attitude and style. But of course they don't want to see the same stories every day. Radio audiences are even keener on consistency, since they may rely on particular 'landmarks' to structure their day. They may, for instance, time their lunchtime to fit in with a particular programme or presenter.

When creating a programme, you are creating the framework that will satisfy the listener's desire for consistency. Several elements are involved.

Programme identity

The programme needs to know who it is. That means it needs a clear idea of who its listeners are and what it will give them. You could even write a little mission statement for a particular programme, which sums up what it will do. The programme will need an appropriate name, which gives an indication of its content, and a signature tune which will be played at various times to remind listeners where they are. The sig tune can also help signal a change of pace or subject within the show.

Tone and attitude

News shows are generally fairly serious, but afternoon shows probably need a slightly more relaxed approach than morning shows. It is also important to decide which intellectual level to pitch the show at. If you run a long, abstract discussion about government financing policies, and then turn to tips on dealing with credit bureaus, the chances are almost all listeners will be turned off by one of the items.

The host

The anchor, presenter or host gives the show its personality and coherence. Geller writes: '(W)hat is unique to each show are the hosts and personalities. That is what the 'other' stations cannot duplicate.'[2] And Robert McLeish says: 'Perhaps the most important single factor in creating a consistent style, the presenter regulates the tone of the programme by his approach to the listener. He or she can be outgoing and friendly, quietly companionable, informal or briskly businesslike, or knowledgeable and authoritative.' This is what 'allows a listener to build a relationship with the programme based on 'liking' and 'trusting'.'[3] In the context of a current affairs show, a presenter should be well-informed, and have a good radio voice and presence. These characteristics will inspire trust among audiences.

Dual presentation costs more, but offers several advantages. It makes for greater variety

Vary the content, but keep the format consistent.

of voices on the show, and allows the station to choose presenters with different strengths. It also maintains more continuity, for the inevitable times when a presenter is away.

Mix

Icasa determines the mix of speech and music a station needs to stick to, but this does not mean every programme has to have the same mix. One programme could be purely speech, the next one only music, and the station can still get the overall proportions right. Current affairs should be mainly speech, but many stations use music to lighten things up.

In designing a programme, some decisions should also be made about the mix of content. Is this programme going to cover only local news? Or must the big international stories always be included? Will there be lifestyle features? And how will they be covered? Are there enough resources to include packages – which take more time and effort to produce, or will the programme rely mainly on telephone interviews? Will there be listener participation in some way? How long should individual items be? These are among the questions that need answering.

Regular features

There are several regular slots that often find their way into a current affairs show. Besides news bulletins, they can include sport, economics, weather, traffic, entertainment and others – anything that listeners need or want to know about regularly. Stations also like to promote programmes coming up later, and may construct editorial features like a weekly personality profile.

Clock

Once these decisions have been taken, it's time to construct the programme's clock, which indicates what will happen at which stage of the programme.

The art of production

Once the show's format has been determined, it needs to be brought alive every day: predictable in its character, surprising in its content. This is the responsibility of the producer, or production team. The presenter, too, can and should play a role in the production effort. For a morning show, production often begins the afternoon before.

Planning

Quality requires planning, which begins with a discussion involving everyone involved in the show. This is the time to brainstorm ideas about what is

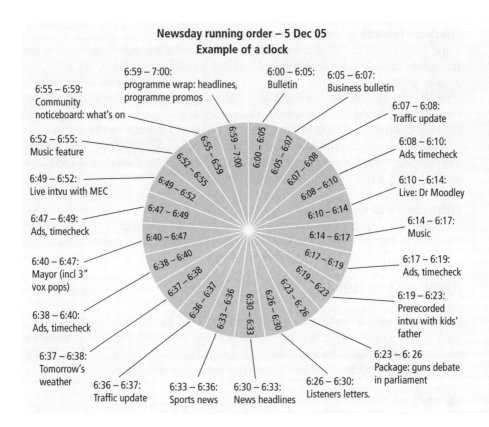

Newsday running order – 5 Dec 05
Example of a clock

6:59 – 7:00: programme wrap: headlines, programme promos

6:55 – 6:59: Community noticeboard: what's on

6:52 – 6:55: Music feature

6:49 – 6:52: Live intvu with MEC

6:47 – 6:49: Ads, timecheck

6:40 – 6:47: Mayor (incl 3" vox pops)

6:38 – 6:40: Ads, timecheck

6:37 – 6:38: Tomorrow's weather

6:36 – 6:37: Traffic update

6:33 – 6:36: Sports news

6:30 – 6:33: News headlines

6:26 – 6:30: Listeners letters.

6:23 – 6:26 Package: guns debate in parliament

6:19 – 6:23: Prerecorded intvu with kids' father

6:17 – 6:19: Ads, timecheck

6:14 – 6:17: Music

6:10 – 6:14: Live: Dr Moodley

6:08 – 6:10: Ads, timecheck

6:07 – 6:08: Traffic update

6:05 – 6:07: Business bulletin

6:00 – 6:05: Bulletin

newsworthy, and how to deal with it. It is important to encourage creative thinking in these discussions. Even an idea that seems crazy or impractical at first may turn into something really worthwhile, or may suggest another idea that flies. But planning sessions can't end there: they need to translate into concrete plans. Everybody involved needs to know what they have to do.

Preparation

There's a lot to be done in preparing to go on air.

Set up interviews

This can be quite difficult, particularly for a morning show. You need to find the right person: somebody who is ready and able to discuss the issue. In talking to that person, the producer will get some idea of their attitude and what kinds of questions will be appropriate. Background research may be necessary – it is essential that the presenter has enough information. A set of questions should be prepared, and a cue sheet written.

Check on incoming material

Some shows may get contributions from people who are not on the core team. These may include a freelancer who files from a small town nearby; or a reporter on a sister station in another centre. The producers will need to check what is coming in from such sources – this may need a phone call, or checking on diaries from elsewhere and commissioning contributions. It may also require a discussion with the contributor to agree on a time for filing and a focus of the report.

The scripts of contributions should be carefully edited before they are put together. And the finished product should be listened to. If an item is broadcast blind, there is a risk of serious embarrassment.

Write cues and links

Each item will need to be introduced, and the links scripted so that the show flows smoothly. It is best if the presenter does this, or at least revises cues others have written, to ensure that the style is her own.

Running order

Each show needs a running order – an indication of the order of items, showing the various lengths. This is a plan of action for everyone involved – technical producer, host, producers and others. The running order will be built around the skeleton that is made up of the show's regular features.

Variety

The programme needs to sound lively and varied. The first thing to consider is the sound of the various items. It is a good idea to arrange them in such a way that different sound quality and different voices alternate. If you have two packages for an hour-long show, you might run one in the first half and one in the second. Interviews over crackly cellphone lines are often hard to hear – running too many close together can try the listeners' patience.

Then there's the question of subject matter. It may be tempting to group stories about a single subject together, but this is not always the best solution. Andrew Boyd points out that research for the British Independent Broadcasting Authority found that listeners are more likely to forget items if they are grouped together. There is a 'meltdown' factor which causes similar stories to run together in people's minds, he says.[5] In addition, it may make sense to spread different takes on a major story throughout the programme in order to make sure that all listeners are provided for, even if they don't stay with the programme for its full length.

In morning shows, the slot just after the 7am news is often the time of the very highest listenership, and is a good place for the lead story

> When you are planning an hour-long news programme you have to keep things strong right the way through, rather than do what happens in a news bulletin, where you start with the most important and finish with the most trivial. It's got to have a strong beginning, to hold itself up in the middle and have a good end. I want a piece that people can remember. – Rob McKenzie, producer/presenter, Capital Radio[4]

of the show. But it does not follow that you rank the items in order of importance – this would lead listeners to expect that the show gets more and more boring as it develops. It's important to space your strong material throughout.

CHECK IT OUT!
- Robert McLeish. Radio production. Oxford: Focal Press, 1998. Chh 15 & 21.
- Andrew Boyd. Broadcast journalism. Oxford: Focal Press, 2002. Chh 11 – 13.

Rhythm and pace
Decisions about the running order will also be affected by these factors. The programme should flow along quickly enough to keep people interested, but it also needs to spend enough time on individual items so that listeners feel they have been given substantial information. 'The style of writing, speed of reading, pace of editing and length of each item determine whether the programme surges ahead or drags,' writes Boyd.[6]

On air

A good current affairs show gives its listeners plenty of signposts. These include frequent timechecks, station and programme identifications. It is also useful to preview items coming up later in the show, to tempt listeners to stay with it for longer. Transitions should be clearly indicated, too, where the programme moves into a different segment, on sport or international news, for instance.

While the show is on air, the producer remains busy. People due to be interviewed live have to be brought into the studio or raised on the telephone. The producer needs to listen closely to the way interviews are going, to suggest to the presenter when they should be ended, and make sure that the next item is ready.

And the producer is responsible for keeping an eye on the clock. If an interview runs longer than intended, something else may need to be dropped or cut short. If the show is running short, there should be something else available that can be dropped in. Fiona Lloyd provides three tips for producers:

- Always have a backup plan
- Be flexible
- Stay cool[7]

Tips for producing current affairs on a shoestring

A good current affairs programme is original, interesting and lively. And you don't need money to have good ideas.

1) Keep a note of story ideas. Whenever you see something that might make a story, write it down. And keep your eyes open.
2) Find ways of discussing ideas with others on the station.
3) Prepare thoroughly for each programme. Do as much background research as possible – that might only mean making some phone calls. Think carefully about the issues you deal with.
4) Rather do a shorter programme well than a longer programme that is not so good.
5) You will probably rely mainly on live interviews. Make them sharp and clear.
6) Still, try to get some packaged material into the programme, even if it's only possible to do so once in a while. Simple vox pop packages don't need much time or resources, and add some different voices to the programme.

DO IT!

1) Listen to AM Live on SAfm, or another current affairs programme. Keep detailed notes of the running order, noting the subject; the kind of item (interview, package etc) and the length. Write some notes about the programme, under the headings used in this chapter, evaluating how successful it is.
2) Write a programme brief for a new current affairs programme on a station. The brief should be about half a page in length, and indicate the name, purpose, time, target audience and editorial brief.
3) Develop a clock for the show, indicating its basic structure and its regular features.
4) Using any information sources you have, draw up a list of items you would include for the show if it was to go out 'today' – the day you are doing this exercise.
5) Draw up the show's running order.
6) Prepare a half-hour studio discussion on a health issue. Outline the plan for the show:
   a. Topic
   b. Participants, and reasons why you have chosen these particular people
   c. An outline of questions
7) If you have access to a studio, record the show.

A discussion programme

A discussion programme involves guests in the studio talking about a particular topic, while listeners may be invited to join in by phone. The host facilitates the discussion.

The format is not a difficult one, but there are pitfalls. It is important to choose the participants well: they should represent different viewpoints on the matter under discussion, and should be able to express their views clearly. There should not be too many: in South Africa's first democratic elections, television and radio debates were held with representatives of every political party – 12 to 15 people. The programmes were unmanageable, since they left individual participants with too little time to speak. And on radio, listeners find it impossible to keep track of who is who if there are too many different voices.

As with a current affairs show, the host needs to be well prepared. She needs to do enough background research to be able to guide the discussion effectively, so that most time is spent on the issues that are important.

It is important to make sure that all viewpoints are heard. No one person should be allowed to dominate, and if somebody is shy, they should be encouraged to participate. The participants should be encouraged to respond to each other.

The host also needs to keep the discussion on track. Digression and irrelevance should be discouraged.

This needs to be done politely and professionally. Be careful to treat all participants equally – if you call one by her first name, and another more formally, it will sound like you favour the first one.

The discussion should flow logically, just like an interview. A plan should be prepared, but should be applied flexibly. It is more important to follow the discussion's organic flow than to impose an artificial structure.

1 Valerie Geller, *Creating Powerful Radio: A Communicator's Handbook*. New York: M Street, 1996. p 53
2 Ibid
3 Robert McLeish, *Radio Production*. Oxford: Focal Press: 1998. p 171
4 Quoted in Andrew Boyd: *Broadcast Journalism* Oxford: Focal Press, 2002, 153
5 Andrew Boyd, *Broadcast Journalism: Techniques for Radio and tTelevision News*. Oxford: Focal Press, 2002. p 152
6 Ibid p 153
7 Fiona Lloyd. *Developing Radio Skills. An Online Course by the International Women's Media Federation*. Posted at http://iwmf.org/training/radio/module3/page9.php. Accessed on 26 October 2005.

A Radio Metro DJ at work, while passing listeners' reflections are picked up in the studio window

Chapter **12**

How to be a radio voice: Presentation

By Noreen Alexander

The ideal radio voice is a natural voice! One that is lively and interesting to listen to, that varies in tone, expression, volume and pace according to the material being delivered. A voice that reflects the passion and involvement of the person talking.

The voice is the key tool of every journalist and presenter on radio. If the listener finds it irritating, boring or unconvincing they will switch off. No audience = no station = no job! The role of a presenter is to communicate ideas and

THE LEARNING CURVE

A Fake Voice

Ace didn't really like the sound of his own voice. He always tried to imitate the presenters he had listened to from childhood. He tried to sound 'beautiful' like they did. He also noticed that their every word sounded crystal clear, and he seemed to sound clearer, too, when he used his lips and tongue a lot. He practised whenever he could, as long as nobody was around. It never sounded quite right, but he kept at it.

One afternoon, he was practising a bulletin script in the production studio. He didn't notice, but Liz had come in and was listening.

"It's good to practise," she said as he finished.

He whirled around. "I ... I didn't know you were there," he stammered.

"You're trying too hard," said Liz. "You actually sound better when you talk normally, then your voice is full and resonant. When you try to 'be a broadcaster', your voice comes from the top of the chest. And you're just making yourself tired by screwing up your face and tongue in that way – you're over-articulating. Just try to speak more normally. You've got a great voice. It's much more important to think about what you are saying than to concentrate so hard on making a different voice for yourself."

Ace took a deep breath and tried again.

"Much better," said Liz with a smile.

information, to talk to a person not 'announce' at them. 'Announcing' is an outdated idea belonging to the early days of radio 50 years ago! There is no place for it in modern broadcasting.

Identity Management

Your voice is very closely linked to your identity. How often have you heard someone say: 'That doesn't sound like my' voice'? All journalists and presenters have a 'professional' identity as well as their personal 'identities' or roles as parents, friends, children and so on. It is important to establish how you want to be 'heard' or perceived by your audience. How do you want them to think of you,

DO IT!

1. List the characteristics you are proud of or like about yourself.
2. Note down the characteristics you would like to show others in your role as a journalist.
3. What characteristics does your audience expect of you as a journalist?
4. Should any of these be added to the characteristics you would like to demonstrate? Add them to the list.
5. Consider how someone demonstrates these characteristics. What would you hear, see or feel? List these criteria by each characteristic.
6. You now have a map to guide you on the kind of behaviours and vocal presentation that will help you communicate using your 'natural' voice.

as reliable or honest or credible or lively or something else? The words you choose to describe yourself or how you would like to be, will help you communicate this persona. It is a self fulfilling prophesy. If we believe we are likeable, enthusiastic and hard working, we usually are and are seen as such by others.

Vocal Myths

In trying to produce a radio voice many people fall into poor vocal habits, sometimes because of incorrect advice from 'experts' who know little about voice production. Two of the most common 'bad habits' are:-

Authority

Sometimes journalists are told to 'sound more authoritative'. As a result they fake an unlikely 'authoritative' sound based upon childhood figures of authority, such as teachers or stern parents. These figures only sounded 'authoritative' when angry! The result is alarming – a sort of irritated, monotonous, mini-shout! Authority lies in the accuracy of the material being presented and the confidence, involvement and understanding of the presenter in delivering it. It does not need to be 'faked'! If you are passionate and believe in what you are saying, the listener will be too.

Every presentation contains key words that reflect the sense of the material. If these words are given the emphasis they need and the less important information is 'thrown away' – given no emphasis – it more accurately represents normal speech. When combined with 'fingerprinting' – reflecting the 'mood' of the material in your tone of voice (happy, sad, funny, serious) – it becomes a true 'communication'.

Projection

Actors need to project their voices so they can be heard at the back of a theatre. But broadcasters have microphones. They do not need to raise the volume of their voices (unless extremely soft spoken). They simply increase the volume

DO IT!

Diaphragmatic breathing
Place your hands just below your ribs.
1. Take in a deep breath and say 'Faa, Faa, Faa, Faa'. Can you feel the diaphragmatic muscle in your stomach moving?
2. Take in a deep breath and laugh. We use our diaphragmatic muscle when we laugh.
3. Lie flat on your back. Place your hands just below your ribs. Draw in a deep breath while counting to 5, then breathe out slowly counting to 6. Do you notice your hands lifting as you breathe in? As you become more practised, you can vary the counts. For example, breathe in to a count of 3 and out to 5 or in to 7 and out to 2. If done regularly, these exercises will help you manage your breathing more effectively and produce a genuine, resonant voice. They have the added bonus of helping you relax.

control on the mike. When broadcasters over-project, they seem to be shouting from a distance. This causes strain on the vocal chords and reduces the range of tone available to them, creating an exciting 'sound picture'. It is very stressful to listen to and distances the listener rather than bringing them into an intimate space where you are talking to them.

Instead of 'projecting', take in a few deep (diaphragmatic) breaths before you start to talk. Continue to breathe deeply during the pauses between ideas. Relax your throat and jaw so the words flow out on a river of air. Speak as loudly as you would when talking to someone a metre away.

Speak to ONE person. Psychologically each listener thinks they are alone with you and it is off-putting to be addressed as if you were in a crowd!

Learning by Imitation
Some people listen to presenters they admire and try to copy them. There is nothing wrong with this – it is a normal way of learning. But it falls down miserably when the person fails to make whatever they have chosen to imitate their own.

The Building Blocks of Presentation

The voice is a communication tool that can be used in many different ways. We can break these down into the building blocks of vocal presentation. The idea is to use your 'natural' voice as effectively as possible. There are very, very few people who have such an unpleasant sounding voice that it needs to change before they can go on air. (If this is the case then perhaps you should consider print journalism rather than broadcast?!)

Pitch
This is the enormous variety of sounds produced by the voice, from very low to very high and everything in between – like music.

In broadcasting your aim is to produce the same variety of pitch as normal speech. The voice goes up and down like music according to what is being said. These variations enhance 'expression' or 'inflection'. When people sound monotonous there's little variety of pitch and the listener's brain switches off.

However too much variation that bears little relationship to the content, ends up sounding like singing and is also a switch off! As a guideline the voice tends to go down at the end of sentences, even though we may choose to emphasise the last word.

Pace

This is one of the biggest challenges facing new presenters. Because they are nervous or want to include more information than the time allows, they speak faster in the mistaken belief that they can cram it all in. The result is incomprehensible to the listener, who needs time to take in what is being said and create thought images. They are still processing your first sentence when you are on the third, so they completely miss the second sentence!

Rather cut a sentence (we won't miss what we haven't heard) and read at your normal speaking pace. For some people this can be quite speedy. The trick is to take slightly longer pauses than you are comfortable with between ideas, so the listener can catch up with you.

If you listen to people talking, you will notice that they vary the pace at which they speak, sometimes fast, sometimes slow. This helps retain interest. Quicken up when presenting less important material and slow down when you reach important ideas.

Pause

On radio, a healthy pause can feel like a lifetime, but it is essential if you are to give the listener time to take in what you are saying. Pauses can also be used just before you communicate an important point. They draw attention to it. Very short or 'hesitation' pauses are also useful when faced with a tricky pronunciation. If you give a very short pause just before you say the word, it gives you time to get your teeth and tongue organised!

Emphasis

A critical tool in the presenter's toolbox! The correct use of emphasis gives meaning to what you are saying. It gives colour and variety. When we are talking we automatically emphasise the appropriate words. We do not even think about it. But something goes wrong when we read. Presenters spend ages wondering whether to emphasise this word or that, instead of thinking about what they want to communicate and trusting themselves to place weight on the key words.

In order to 'speak' a script though, you need to have written a 'spoken' script. One that reads just as you would speak, not a literary masterpiece! It is much harder, if not impossible to emphasise key words and 'throw-away' the rest, if the script

Many broadcasters decorate their scripts with all kinds of graphics indicating when to pause or emphasise. Effectively they then switch off when presenting and obey the marks. At first you may need to mark pause and emphasis just to remind yourself, but get out of the habit as soon as you can. Then you can THINK about what you are saying and you will naturally pause and emphasise correctly.

is for the eye. A 'written' script is pretty well always 'read' rather than 'talked'.

Overusing or underusing emphasis confuses the listener. They are not sure what to pay attention to and eventually the effort of trying to understand becomes too much and they stop listening!

Volume

As we saw earlier, shouting into the microphone has no place in modern broadcast journalism.

Research suggests that

- when people listen to the radio they imagine they are in the same space as the person talking, which means that even if they are on the other side of the room from the radio, they 'hear' the presenter as if they were no more than one metre away;
- most people listen to radio as a background activity and only pay attention when a word or phrase captures their interest. They listen to patterns of information and scan for these key words which are signalled by a change in vocal tone;
- listeners choose their favourite presenters using the same criteria they use for choosing friends![1]

It is important then to use your normal volume when presenting. This will vary as it does in speech, for example, louder when you are excited or softer when thoughtful.

This variety is important because it lends interest to what you are saying. A continuous shout or a continuous whisper simply puts the listener to sleep!

Involvement

If you are involved and thinking about what you are saying while you are saying it all these building blocks tend to fall into place naturally. This is a skill like all the others. Often broadcasters worry far too much about HOW they are saying something rather than WHAT they are saying.

Ten user-friendly habits
- Speak at your normal pace
- Using your normal voice
- At its normal volume
- Think about what you are saying
- Be interested in the topic
- Write as you speak
- Read your script aloud when writing and again when you have finished
- Vary the pace, the pauses and emphasis
- Match the tone of your voice to the content
- Speak to ONE person – never say 'listeners' or 'all you out there'
- Relax
- Breathe!

Preparation

Whether you are presenting a script you have written or someone else's, you will need to read through it aloud at least once before presenting, so you can check on unfamiliar names and pronunciations and any awkward phrases you might fluff on.

For some people reading through the script once is enough, others need two or three 'reads' before feeling ready to present. How many times do you need to read through your own script or someone else's?

Always check the pronunciation of unfamiliar names. Incorrect pronunciations destroy your credibility. After all, if you don't even know how to say the name, how can we be sure you have your facts right?

It is important to read aloud when preparing. We always read perfectly in our heads. It is only when we read aloud that we discover any difficulties.

Fluffing

Many newcomers to broadcasting consider 'fluffing' or tripping over a word to be a major crime and tie themselves in knots trying to avoid it. They judge the success or otherwise of their presentation by the number of fluffs they have made.

As a result their whole presentation is affected by fear or the anticipation of fluffing. The reality is we all fluff sometimes. It is perfectly natural to fluff. And unless you fluff in every single sentence do not worry about it!

The framework of fluffing

Fluffing usually happens when we read too far ahead and our short term memory fails. There are several ways of controlling this. Two of the most common are:

DO IT!
Facial gym
1. Squeeze your face, eyes and mouth into a tight 'prune'.
2. Stretch your face, eyes and mouth as wide as you can.
3. Swing the lower jaw from side to side.
4. Stretch the mouth as wide open as you can and say 'AHHHHH'.
5. Stretch the eyes open and squeeze them shut.
6. Put your tongue out as far as it can go, touch your nose, chin, cheeks.
7. Flap your tongue in and out of your mouth as fast as you can.
8. Gently rest your right ear on top of your right shoulder. Do the same on the left.
9. Gently rest your chin on your chest, then the back of your head on the back of your neck.
10. Breathe!

- Take a blank sheet of paper and place it just below the line you are reading, only move it to the next line when you have read about 2/3 of the way through the first. You can also use a finger, a pencil or a ruler to do this.

CHECK IT OUT!
- Robert McLeish: Radio Production, Ch 8

- When reading, look up between each piece of information.

If you tend to fluff on difficult words or names try:-
- Writing the correct pronunciation in a way you will understand, above the word.
- Break long words into small chunks and write above the long word.

It is a waste of time and energy worrying about what may happen, such as worrying about a possible fluff. Rather use that energy to trust yourself and your ability to manage any difficulties that may arise.

If you do fluff, do not allow it to affect the rest of your presentation. Often when people fluff, they spend the rest of the story thinking about the fluff and not what they are saying. As a result that one small mistake has an awful effect on their whole presentation. Chances are the listener never even noticed the fluff, but they will certainly notice if the rest of the story is affected!

Relaxation
It is natural to feel some tension when you first start broadcasting and this can become a problem if it becomes a 'habit'. Tension affects your breathing and your voice. When you are nervous the muscles in your throat, neck and jaw tighten. Sometimes this feels as though you have a 'frog' in your throat or it can cause your voice to become 'cracked' or squeaky.
Use diaphragmatic breathing to help you relax. Avoid taking drinks that are too hot, too cold or milky before presenting. They affect the vocal chords.
Use facial and physical relaxation exercises. Think about what you are saying not the difficulty you may have in saying it!

1 Tony Schwartz, *The Responsive Chord*. Anchor Press: 1973.

Chapter **13**

Responsibilities

The discussion about responsibilities begins with the constitution, which contains
a bill of rights guaranteed to all members of society. Among those rights is one
that is particularly important and precious to journalists. It's worth quoting in
full:

1. Everyone has the right to freedom of expression, which includes
   a. freedom of the press and other media;
   b. freedom to receive or impart information or ideas;
   c. freedom of artistic creativity; and
   d. academic freedom and freedom of scientific research.
2. The right in subsection (1) does not extend to
   a. propaganda for war;
   b. incitement of imminent violence; or

THE LEARNING CURVE

A Beginning

It was late. Lerato was finishing a script she had been working on, while Ace was sorting through some papers. Everybody else had gone home.

"You know, I don't think we should have played that track on the show. It really was filthy," said Ace thoughtfully. It was the story of the week: a local musician who called himself Baddy B had recorded a track that was full of obscenities. The churches had condemned the artist, and had even sent a delegation to Sandi FM to demand that the station stop playing it. It was a tough decision, since teenagers loved it, and the station was keen on supporting local musicians. In the end, though, the station manager had given in and pulled the song.

Lerato turned on him: "Don't be stupid. Don't you know there's a difference between playing something as music and playing it so that people know what they are talking about? Why don't you just think for a bit, instead of always trying to know everything?"

Now he was angry. Both of them were on their feet, facing each other hotly. "Don't call me stupid. You're the one who always thinks she knows everything. I can't believe I ever thought we ..." and he broke off.

"We what?" she asked sharply.

"Never mind."

Both of them returned to what they were doing. Lerato erased a paragraph. Ace straightened some papers.

"Sorry," he said. "I didn't mean it."

"I'm sorry, too."

He shuffled some more papers. "I just do think that many people were offended, even if the song was being discussed on the show."

"It's true. It's a foul song. But we can't protect listeners from everything that might be unpleasant. And you can't really discuss something unless you know what you're talking about. People are so quick to complain about songs, without even hearing them. And their own kids are listening to this stuff!"

Ace thought about what she had said. "I suppose so," he said slowly.

And then Lerato was next to him, turning his face and kissing him, long and soft on the lips.

"What's that about?" he said as soon as he could.

"You try so hard – work, me. It's very sweet. You've learned a lot since you got here, even that it's OK to be wrong sometimes." She paused. "Are you still interested in going out? Today's Friday...."

Ace grinned at her. Things were turning out better than fine.

c. advocacy of hatred that is based on race, ethnicity, gender or religion, and that constitutes incitement to cause harm.[1]

Freedom of expression guarantees everyone the right to say and write pretty much what they like. It is enormously important to journalists because it underpins pretty much everything we do.

It is also central to the idea of democracy. If citizens don't have access to reasonably reliable information, democracies can't function. People need to

RADIO JOURNALISM TOOLKIT

128

The pressure group Reporters without Borders releases an annual report ranking countries according to their level of press freedom. In the 2005 report, Nordic countries like Denmark and Sweden again scored highest. Benin, Namibia, Cape Verde and South Africa are the best African countries, all in the top 35 and ahead of the US. North Korea, Eritrea and Turkmenistan come in at the bottom. The group says about these countries: 'Journalists there simply relay government propaganda. Anyone out of step is harshly dealt with. A word too many, a commentary that deviates from the official line or a wrongly-spelled name and the author may be thrown in prison or draw the wrath of those in power. Harassment, psychological pressure, intimidation and round-the-clock surveillance are routine.'

Check out the full report at http://www.rsf.org/rubrique.php3?id_rubrique=554

know when the petrol price is going up, where the taxi routes are and what their political choices are: what parties are promising to do for them, what their record is and so on. Otherwise, the right to vote is meaningless.

Media freedom is primarily the right to be informed. Journalists use it every day, and do well to remember that they do so on behalf of the public, and more particularly their specific audiences. Societies tolerate their embarrassing questions on the basis that they supply a crucial service: information.

We should not be starry-eyed about it. Around the world, journalists are often in the firing line. They have been killed in Somalia, kidnapped in Iraq and jailed in the US.

Having emerged from the apartheid era where media freedom was extremely limited, South Africans can be proud of their more recent record. Nevertheless, there are always pressures. There are still disputes with the authorities about issues like Section 205 of the Criminal Procedures Act, which has been used to compel journalists to testify in court. And there is constant pressure from political and commercial interests to make journalists follow a particular line. Sometimes these take the form of friendly inducements – free lunches and the like. Sometimes they involve threats and court cases.

In this difficult environment, journalists need to hold onto two things. The first is that their foremost loyalty is to their audiences. If there is public interest in an issue, other considerations must come second. The second is that journalistic ethics are a compass to help them deal with the dilemmas that arise. We will consider some of the specific ethical principles later in this chapter.

The law

Despite the importance of freedom of speech, it is not absolute. The law lays down some areas where it has to give way to other rights. It is impossible here to do justice to the complicated area of media law, and unfortunately the most recent book on the subject – Kelsey Stuart's Newspaperman's Guide to the Law – is hopelessly out of date. Any newsroom should have fast and reliable access to a lawyer who knows a bit about the field, so that any issues can be dealt with quickly. Individual journalists can't be expected to have specialised knowledge of the area, but should know enough so that they can alert an editor or station manager of a potential problem. This discussion will simply identify some of the possible problem areas.

Defamation

When you publish or broadcast something that harms somebody's reputation, like Mr X is a rapist, or the mayor accepted a bribe, it is known as defamation. Somebody can be defamed by a statement, but also by photographs, cartoons etc. A person can be defamed, and so can a company or other organisation. A journalist, publication, radio station etc can be sued for defamation. People are quick to threaten court action, but don't often really go through with it.

There are ways for a news organisation to defend itself against a defamation suit. Most commonly, this would involve an argument that the statement was true and in the public interest.

This means journalists should make very sure of their facts. If the matter comes to court, you may be called upon to prove the story, or at least that you did your utmost to make sure of the facts. It's particularly important to make sure you give the person involved a chance to respond.

To defend themselves against a defamation case, journalists also have to show that there was real public interest in the matter. This means they need to show that the report does not simply satisfy public curiosity, but that citizens have a reason for needing to know.

Statements made in Parliament and in courts are privileged: you can't be sued for defamation if you report statements made there even if they would have been defamatory under other circumstances. Also, statements regarded as 'fair comment' can also be made without becoming defamatory, eg the Minister of Housing is not doing her job.

Courts

There are a number of laws that affect reporting of matters before court. The sub judice principle says that you can't publish or broadcast anything that may have the effect of interfering with the administration of justice. Contravening this principle may leave the journalist in contempt of court. Examples include:

- Immoderate criticism of the court (but more reasonable criticism has become OK)
- Revealing the contents of documents before they've been handed in to court
- Speculating about the outcome of a case
- Contravening an order of court that protects the identity of a witness or certain evidence
- Reporting on information obtained outside the court which might influence the court

The sub judice rule is much abused by officials who don't want to talk: it really only applies to matters in court or before some commissions. It doesn't apply to matters being investigated internally, for instance, or where a charge has been laid.

You can't identify children (under 18) who are accused, witnesses or victims in a criminal case. This means you can't use their names, and also can't give any details that may identify them (the name of their mother, their address, etc).

You can't identify an accused before they have been formally charged in court.

You can't report the details of a divorce case, except the names of the people involved, the fact that they are getting divorced, and the outcome.

You also can't identify the complainant in a case involving rape or sexual assault, or the accused until the trial begins.

Section 205 of the Criminal Procedures Act says that a person who has evidence of a crime can be forced to testify on it. That includes journalists. But journalist ethics prevent them from identifying a source, and many have gone to jail rather than testify. This became an issue in the Staggie case, arising out of the murder of a Cape gang leader. Journalists have argued that forcing them to testify puts them in danger, and harms their reputation of impartiality.

Privacy

The common law and the Constitution protect a person's privacy. This means you can't bug phones, quote from private documents, tape phone conversations without consent, take somebody's photograph without consent and the like. This can only be overridden in cases of overwhelming public interest.

Access to Information

Relatively new legislation gives the public – including journalists – access to official and other information. There are some exceptions, like issues involving doctor-patient confidentiality; things affecting national security and a few others. But in many cases reporters now have the right to insist that officials make information available to them.

Ethics

When a young reporter on the New York Times named Jayson Blair was caught out inventing stories and sources, he wrecked his own career and damaged a great newspaper. Ultimately, senior editors on the paper had to resign because of the scandal. They were seen as responsible for allowing significant harm to the paper's credibility, its most precious asset.

Ethics underpin the relationship of trust news media have with their audiences. Jovial Rantao, the editor of the Sunday Independent, writes: 'Credibility is the lifeblood of our profession as journalists. Credibility is to us what oxygen is to the

Law and ethics

Media law has an either-or approach. Either you obey the law or you do not. If you do not obey the law, there are punitive consequences or sanctions imposed by courts of law. ... A law does not say how a reporter ought to behave; it merely states what the minimum standards of behaviour are. When we start using words like 'should' and 'ought', we are talking about ethics. – Francois Nel[2]

human body. Without it, we are nothing. Without it, not one person will believe one single word that we write. One of the basic tenets of our profession is to ensure that the credibility of the information we gather on a daily basis is unquestionable.'[3]

Four principles

A very influential trio of ethical principle was developed at the Poynter Institute in the US. They are
• truthtelling, which includes accuracy and fairness;
• independence; and
• minimising harm.
I would add a fourth: accountability.

CHECK IT OUT!
• Franz Krüger, Black, white and grey – Ethics in South African journalism. Cape Town: Double Storey, 2004.
• Johan Retief, Media ethics. Cape Town: Oxford University Press, 2002.
• The website www.journalism. co.za has an ethics page called journ-ethics, containing codes of conduct, scenarios and other materials.
• Guidelines on covering AIDS can be found at http://www. journaids.org/ethics.php

But should we pay any attention to standards developed in the US? Zambian academic Francis Kasoma has argued that African journalists should look to their own moral heritage, which would make for kinder journalism. 'There is too much of the cold Euro-American brand of news reporting in Africa ... Africa has the chance to restore the human touch to journalism,' he writes.[4]

This is an important debate, but I have argued elsewhere[5] that the basic principles apply across cultures: truthtelling, for instance is a value that is fundamental to all societies. The way these fundamental values are applied, however, will depend on the context, and in fact changes from time to time.

Accuracy

Getting it right is fundamental to journalism. Listeners care deeply about the small things. A survey of American attitudes quotes respondents as saying: 'Those two streets don't even intersect. How could two cars collide there?' and 'That's not even the correct name for that hospital: I know because my sister works there.'[6] It is simply essential to get the facts right.

Journalists have to deal with very complex issues: the science of AIDS treatment, unemployment statistics or international trade issues. Although we can't be specialists in all these fields, we need to make sure we know enough so that we don't make stupid mistakes. There is an ethical obligation to be smart, as Bob Steele of the Poynter Institute puts it.[7]

Accuracy requires that we take great care in editing somebody's words. It is not acceptable to change the speaker's meaning or intention – and this means we have to include any qualifications she may have expressed.

Accuracy demands that we pronounce the names of people or places correctly. In our multi-lingual country, reporters and newsreaders are often confronted with unfamiliar names. It is important to make an effort to get the names right, and that includes the clicks of Xhosa or the guttural 'g' of Afrikaans. While there is some understanding when people struggle with difficult sounds, there can be no excuse for things like inserting an 'a' into the President's name, turning him into Thabo Mabeki.

Related is the question of dialect. English, particularly, is spoken in many different ways around the world. It belongs to everyone, and many different dialects should be acceptable. As long as the words are understandable, there should be fairly wide acceptance of different versions of English. However, it is not always easy to draw the line between accent and outright mispronunciation. And audiences are often very sensitive to language 'purity'.

Fairness

Fairness belongs under the heading of truthtelling because leaving out the 'other side' of the story leaves it incomplete, and is therefore misleading. If somebody is accused of corruption, it's only fair to give them the chance to state their case.

It is important to give them a real chance to respond. A journalistic investigation may take quite a long time, sometimes months or years. It would be unfair to contact the person at the very last minute, perhaps leaving a message on a cellphone, and then go on air with the story.

This does not mean that the person can hold the station to ransom by refusing to respond, or taking an unreasonable amount of time to come up with a comment. If you feel the person has been given enough time and opportunity and is not taking it, there's no reason to hold the story back.

Live broadcasting can pose particular dangers, in that a caller or interviewee may unexpectedly come out with defamatory accusations. A producer screening calls can try to prevent this happening, but calls can still slip past. Stations used to have a time delay on broadcast – if something defamatory or offensive was said, a button was hit before the words reached the air, and listeners were given music to listen to for a bit. But these are now rare, and most live shows really are completely live.

If something is unexpectedly said that demands a response, it is important to get that response as soon as possible.

Independence

In 2003, it emerged that the editor of City Press, Vusi Mona, was running a public relations firm that was doing work for the Mpumalanga government. His company investigated the situation, and he had to leave his job. It was clear that his independence had been compromised. His involvement in the PR company created a conflict of interest, since his editorial decisions might have been shaped by his business relationship. If the paper had run a positive story on Mpumalanga, readers would have been unsure how seriously to take it. In other words, it affected the paper's credibility.

Conflicts of interest can arise in many areas. They can be business related, like Mona's case. They can also be personal, where we find ourselves covering a story involving a person to whom we are related. If that happens, it is usually best to pass on the story to a colleague. And they can be political, which is why journalists generally stay away from active party politics.

Independence also means that journalists should not get involved in the story. They are there to observe events, not make them. It is obviously inappropriate for a journalist covering a riot to start throwing stones, or to help the police make arrests.

But that brings us to an area where things become more difficult. There are areas where a journalist's duties conflict with the general duties of citizens, such as where we end up with information that could help put a criminal behind bars. We have already touched on Section 205 of the Criminal Procedures Act. In general, journalists' independence is so important that they want to retain an arm's length relationship, even with the state.

Commercial pressures on the media have become huge. It is tough to run a story exposing bad employment practices at a shopping centre that is an important advertiser. Suppressing a story because we don't want to risk losing an advertising contract may save us that money – but we will pay in credibility.

Freebies have become a major feature of journalism, with everything from a free cup of coffee and pens to cellphones and overseas trips being available to journalists. There are always strings attached. Many newsrooms have clear policies about how they should be handled.

The source

The relationship with our sources is a complicated one. On the one hand, we treat them with some scepticism. We are always cross-checking the information we get, and wondering about their motives for talking to us. At the same time, a measure of trust is needed on both sides.

We owe our sources a great deal. Without them, we would have nothing to report. In return, we owe them honesty and consideration.

One of the best known rules of journalism ethics is that sources are protected. The reason is simple: sources have been dismissed or otherwise harmed, some have even been killed for talking to journalists, and we have a responsibility to protect them from any retribution.

This most often means keeping their identity secret, and some journalists have

How do you knock when there's no door? ... Without the paraphernalia of the powerful – the gatekeepers and spindoctors, the officialese and the threat of legal censure – it is up to us to ensure privacy rights of the poor. For me, this means asking for permission to take photographs every time. It means setting up interviews with local community leaders who will introduce you to members of the community. You would not arrive at Anglo American unannounced or just walk into Reserve Bank Governor Tito Mboweni's office. The same rules should apply in grassroote reporting.
– Ferial Haffajee, editor of the Mail&Guardian[8]

gone to jail rather than name a source. Because they are taken so seriously, promises of this kind should not be given lightly, and it is important that both sides are completely clear on what is being agreed on.

Particular issues arise when the people you are talking to are unused to the media or otherwise vulnerable. When you are dealing with the bereaved family of somebody who has died in a taxi accident, for instance, it is important not to exploit their vulnerability. Particular care should be taken when talking to children.

Privacy

The constitution and the law protect a person's privacy, and this can only be overridden if there is very clear public interest. Two areas arise: the one involves intrusion, where journalists enter somebody's private space without permission. This also includes the use of telephoto lenses or recording equipment.

You should ask people for permission before recording a telephone interview, particularly if you intend to use the material for broadcast. People need to know they are speaking in public.

Famous people have slightly reduced rights to privacy. Their lives have become public property. So when Nelson Mandela got divorced, the media covered the case in detail even though the law restricts coverage of divorce. Even famous people retain some privacy, though, and it is sometimes not easy to find the right balance. The editor of *The Star*, Moegsien Williams, said: 'The rule of thumb for me is if Minister So-and-so is drunk over the weekend in his lounge at home, it is his business. If Minister So-and-so is drunk on a Wednesday in his office, it's my business.'[9]

DO IT!
1. Have a look at your station's licence application. What promises were made? What is its mission statement?
2. Discuss the following questions:
   a. Do you think African journalists should develop their own standards?
   b. A prominent musician dies after a long illness at the age of 31. A close friend (who does not want to be named) tells you he died of AIDS, but his family says it was pneumonia. Do you report what you heard from the friend?
   c. The police raid a hotel in Hillbrow and arrest 15 alleged drug dealers. They say 12 of them are Nigerians. Does your report mention the nationality of the people held?
   d. Sipho Zondi, an ANC election candidate, calls in to your show, and says live on air that David Mkhwanazi, a candidate for the UDM, stole money from the school where Mkhwanazi is the headmaster. What do you do?

Causing offence

Many people are concerned with the portrayal of sex, violence, nudity, bad language. This is more of an issue with television and newspaper images, but there have been instances where lewd material or swearing drew criticism on radio.

Broadcasters need to have good reason for using this kind of material. It can be justified if there is a real journalistic purpose to it. But it should not be included just for the sake of shocking listeners. In early 2002, the playwright Mbongeni Ngema released a CD with the song AmaNdiya – The Indians. The song was widely condemned as anti-Indian and racist, and a complaint was lodged with the BCCSA when Ukhozi FM played extracts of the song to lead into a discussion about the issue. The song amounted to hate speech and should not have been played, the complainant argued. The commission agreed that it was hate speech, but said that playing it to introduce a discussion was justified. It was an example of where even extremely offensive material could be used for journalistic purposes.

Accountability

Accepting accountability does not mean that journalists allow others to dictate what they should do. It means simply that they are prepared to explain and answer for their actions, both in their dealings with listeners and with bodies like the BCCSA.

The situation is complex for community radio stations, who hold themselves accountable to the people they serve. It is an admirable principle – but it has to be balanced with the journalist's need to remain independent. Community accountability cannot mean broadcasting whatever the civic association wants to have on air, and by implication suppressing the things they don't want to hear. Accountability must be to the community as a whole, and that requires independence from particular groups, even democratically elected ones.

The question of public interest

Journalists often use the notion of public interest to decide whether it is OK to infringe somebody's rights. For instance, journalistic ethics would say that our newsgathering techniques should normally be open and honest. But there may be

The public interest is the only test that justifies departure from the highest standards of journalism and includes:
a. detecting or exposing crime or serious misdemeanour;
b. detecting or exposing serious anti-social conduct;
c. protecting public health and safety;
d. preventing the public from being misled by some statement or action of an individual or organisation;
e. detecting or exposing hypocrisy, falsehoods or double standards or behaviour on the part of public figures or institutions and in public institutions.
- SA Press Code of Conduct

occasions where we could uncover crime by recording people secretly. In such a situation, we would need to argue that there was a real need for the public to be informed, and that this need was more important than the rights of the people we were reporting on.

Public interest is not a precisely defined idea, even though there is a useful definition in the Press Code of Conduct (see box.) It can be abused by editors who want to find excuses for something. But it remains a crucial notion, which we use all the time.

Tips for law & ethics on a shoestring

Principles can be expensive. Running a story about bad meat being sold at a supermarket may lose the station an important advertising contract. But not running it is also expensive: it will lose the station credibility among its listeners. And that is ultimately more important.

Freebies that come into community stations staffed by volunteers can cause real difficulties. Some years ago, a company gave many stations several microwave ovens each, to hand out to listeners as prizes. Many staff members found it impossible to resist them, and found various ways of making sure they got their share. It is important for stations to develop a clear policy on how they will deal with situations like this. One station kept one microwave for the office, and handed out the rest – probably an acceptable compromise.

It is important not to become dependent on news sources. If a political party gives you a ride to their rally, you may be compromised. And if you don't cover the other party because they didn't offer a lift, your coverage has become unbalanced. Newsrooms need to have enough resources to be able to do their work independently.

Legal advice can also be costly. It is a good idea to have a lawyer on the board of a community station, who may be willing to give free advice in sticky situations. There are also Legal Resource Centres and university legal aid clinics who may be able to help.

1   *The Constitution of the Republic of South Africa*, 1996.
2   Francois Nel, *Writing for the Media in Southern Africa*. Cape Town, Oxford University Press: 2005. 334
3   The Star, 10 May 2002
4   Francis Kasoma, *An Introduction to Journalism Ethical Reasoning in Africa*, in:Francis Kasoma (ed) *Journalism Ethics in Africa*. Nairobi: Acce, 1994. p 34
5   Franz Krüger, *Black, White and Grey: Ethics in South African Journalism*. Cape Town: Double Storey, 2004. pp 9 - 12.
6   Robert J. Haiman. (undated). *Best Practices for Newspaper Journalists*. Freedom Forum. Posted at http://www.freedomforum.org/publications/diversity/bestpractices/bestpractices.pdf Accessed on 19 March 2004
7   Borrowed from the title of a *"Talk about Ethics"* column by Bob Steele, 9 July 2002. Posted at http://www.poynter.org/column.asp?id=36&aid=785 Accessed on 19 March 2004
8   Ferial Haffajee: *How do you knock when there's no door?* In: Franz Krüger, *Black, White and Grey: Ethics in South African Journalism*. Cape Town: Double Storey, 2004. 201
9   Quoted in Krüger, op cit, p 196

Glossary: Radio journalism vocabulary

Note: The use of radio terms varies widely in different news organisations and countries. Underlined terms are defined separately. The entries marked with an asterisk (*) come from training notes prepared by the Australian Broadcasting Corporation in 1994.

Actuality: Piece of sound material that has been recorded in the field.

Anchor: Also known as host or presenter; a person who presents a radio show.

Ambient sound: Also known as atmos, fx, or natural sound; background sound from the location of a recording, eg traffic noise. It is used to create atmosphere.

Angle: An aspect of a news report that the reporter chooses to focus on.

Atmos: Another term for ambient sound.

Back announcement: Details of an item, such as the name of the reporter, given immediately afterwards.

Bed: Background music or jingle used underneath a voice. *

Breaking story: A news event that is reported as it happens.

Bridge: Music or sound effects used to link one item to another. *

Bulletin: News summary, usually at the top of the hour.

Cans: Headphones.

Clip: Also known as sound bite; a short piece of sound cut from an interview with a source.

Cross-face: Fading one sound out as another sound is faded in. *

Cue: Also known as intro; a short introduction to a news report or piece, read by the presenter.

Cue sheet: Document giving a show's running order, cues and technical information.

Current affairs programme: Longer form news programme.

Dead air: Silence during a radio programme. *

Deadline: The time by which material must be prepared. *

Decibel (dB): Measurement of the level of sound. *

Desk: Studio control panel.

Dub: Copy a piece of sound.

Fade: Decrease or increase in volume.

Fader: A device to control the level of sound. *

Feature: (1) Another term for a package.

(2) A slot that appears regularly in a programme and is dedicated to a particular subject, eg economics, film reviews or a traffic update.

Feedback: Also known as howlback; the terrible noise that results when a microphone picks up the output from a speaker and feeds it back to itself.

Fx: Another term for ambient sound.

Hard copy: A text-only news report that will be read by the news presenter.

Host: Another term for anchor.

Illustrated report: Another term for a package.

Insert: Live or recorded segments within a programme. *

Jack: Male plug for input of a signal into a tape recorder or other audio equipment. *

Links: Also known as tracks; the narration, read by the reporter, that 'link' the different soundbites in an item.

Live: Discussion, interview or other event that is broadcast as it happens.

Live crossing: When a journalist reports live from the scene of an event, the show is said to 'cross live' to him or her.

Mix: The blending of two sounds.

Mixer: Equipment with various inputs, which can be selected or blended when recording, editing or broadcasting. *

Monitor: 1) A loudspeaker to listen to programme or sound material. *

2) (As a verb) To listen to a programme with a particular purpose. *

Natural sound: Another term for ambient sound.

News peg: An event or recent development that is used to 'hang' a report about a particular issue on.

OB: Outside broadcast.

Package: Also known as illustrated report or feature; a longer report, with clips, mostly used in current affairs programmes.

Pitch: When a reporter presents an idea for a story, s/he is said to 'pitch' it. Can also be used as a noun.

Presenter: Another term for host.

Pre-recorded: Item is recorded for later broadcast.

Q&A: Also known as a two-way; an interview that is broadcast as such, with questions and answers alternating. It may be pre-recorded and edited, or broadcast live.

Running order: The sequence of items in a programme.

Running story: A story that keeps on generating newsworthy developments.

Scene-setter: A report that 'sets the scene' for an imminent news event.

Signoff: Also known as the standard outcue (SOQ); at the end of a radio news report, the reporter signs off by giving his or her name, identifying the station and saying where s/he is.

Slug: The name given a script or written story for quick identification, like a computer filename (these days, the slug is often simply the filename).

Soundbite: Another term for a clip.

Spot: An advertisement on radio.

Standard outcue (or SOQ): Another term for a signoff.

Talent: Somebody who is being interviewed for radio.

Talkback: A programme that listeners can participate in by phone. *

Tracks: Another term for links.

Two-way: Another term for a Q&A.

Voicer: A news report that is spoken by the reporter (rather than read by the presenter.)

Vox pop: A series of recorded comments from the public, usually recorded in a public place and then edited together.

Appendix 1
Icasa code of conduct for broadcasters

Foreword

1. Section 2 of the Independent Broadcasting Authority Act No. 153 of 1993 ("the Act") enjoins the Independent Broadcasting Authority ("the Authority") to ensure that broadcasting licensees adhere to a Code of Conduct acceptable to the Authority.
2. In terms of section 56(1) of the Act, "all broadcasting licensees shall adhere to the Code of Conduct for Broadcasting Services as set out in Schedule 1." The provisions of that sub- section do not, however, apply to any broadcasting licensee "if he or she is a member of a body which has proved to the satisfaction of the Authority that its members subscribe and adhere to a Code of Conduct enforced by that body by means of its own disciplinary mechanism, and provided that such Code of Conduct and disciplinary mechanisms are acceptable to the Authority".

Definitions

3. "audience" as referred to in this Code means a visual and an aural audience i.e. both television and radio audiences. "broadcasts intended for adult audiences" as referred to in this Code means broadcasts depicting excessive violence and explicit sexual conduct and shall exclude broadcasts intended for children. "children" as referred to in this Code means those persons below 16 years. "watershed period" as referred to in this Code means the period between 21h00 and 05h00. Such restriction applies only to television services.

Preamble

4. Freedom of expression lies at the foundation of a democratic South Africa and is one of the basic pre-requisites for this country's progress and the development in liberty of every person. Freedom of expression is a condition indispensable to the attainment of all other freedoms. The premium our Constitution attaches to freedom of expression is not novel; it is an article of faith in the democracies of the kind we are venturing to create.
5. Constitutional protection is afforded to freedom of expression in section 16 of the Constitution which provides:
   "(1) Everyone has the right to freedom of expression, which includes -
   (a) Freedom of the press and other media;
   (b) Freedom to receive or impart information or ideas;
   (c) Freedom of artistic creativity; and

(d) Academic freedom and freedom of scientific research.

(2) The right in sub-section (1) does not extend to -

(a) Propaganda for war;

(b) Incitement of imminent violence; or

(c) Advocacy of hatred that is based on race, ethnicity, gender or religion, and that constitutes incitement to cause harm."

6. Whilst in most democratic societies freedom of expression is recognised as being absolutely central to democracy, in no country is freedom of expression absolute. Like all rights freedom of expression is subject to limitation under section 36 of the Constitution.

7. The outcome of disputes turning on the guarantee of freedom of expression will depend upon the value the courts are prepared to place on that freedom and the extent to which they will be inclined to subordinate other rights and interests to free expression. Rights of free expression will have to be weighed up against many other rights, including the right to equality, dignity, privacy, political campaigning, fair trial, economic activity, workplace democracy, property and most significantly the rights of children and women.

8. In the period prior to the transition to democracy, governmental processes neither required nor welcomed the adjuncts of free expression and critical discussion and our country did not treasure at its core a democratic ideal. The right to freedom of expression was regularly violated with impunity by the legislature and the executive. Therefore the protection of this right is of paramount importance now that South Africa is grappling with the process of purging itself of those laws and practices from our past which do not accord with the values which underpin the Constitution.

Application of the Code

9. All licensees are required to ensure that all broadcasts comply with this Code and are further required to satisfy the Authority that they have adequate procedures to fulfil this requirement. All licensees should ensure that relevant employees and programme-makers, including those from whom they commission programmes, understand the Code's contents and significance. All licensees should also have in place procedures for ensuring that programme-makers can seek guidance on the Code within the licensee's organisation at a senior level.

10. While the Authority is responsible for drafting this Code of Conduct and for monitoring compliance therewith, independent producers or others supplying programme material should seek guidance on specific proposals from the relevant licensee.

11. Under the Act, the Authority has the power to impose sanctions, including fines, on licensees who do not comply with this Code of Conduct.

12. This Code does not attempt to cover the full range of programme matters with which the Authority and licensees are concerned. This is not because such matters are insignificant, but because they have not given rise to the need for Authority guidance. The Code is therefore not a complete guide to good practice in every situation. Nor is it necessarily the last word on the matters to which it refers. Views and attitudes

change, and any prescription for what is required of those who make and provide programmes may be incomplete and may sooner or later become outdated. The Code is subject to interpretation in the light of changing circumstances, and in some matters it may be necessary, from time to time, to introduce fresh requirements.

13. In drawing up this Code the Authority has taken into account the objectives of the Act and the urgent need in South Africa for the fundamental values which underlie our legal system to accommodate to the norms and principles which are embraced by our Constitution.

Violence

14 Licensees shall not broadcast any material which judged within context:-
(i) contains gratuitous violence in any form i.e. violence which does not play an integral role in developing the plot, character or theme of the material as a whole.
(ii) sanctions, promotes or glamorizes violence.

15. Violence against women
Broadcasters shall:-
(i) not broadcast material which, judged within context, sanctions, promotes or glamorizes any aspect of violence against women ;
(ii) ensure that women are not depicted as victims of violence unless the violence is integral to the story being told;
(iii) be particularly sensitive not to perpetuate the link between women in a sexual context and women as victims of violence.

16. Violence against specific groups
16.1 Licensees shall not broadcast material which, judged within context sanctions, promotes or glamorizes violence based on race, national or ethnic origin, colour, religion, gender, sexual orientation, age, or mental or physical disability.
16.2 Licensees are reminded generally of the possible dangers of some people imitating violence details of which they see, hear or read about.

17 The abovementioned prohibitions shall not apply to -
(i) a bona fide scientific, documentary, dramatic, artistic, or religious broadcast, which judged within context, is of such nature;
(ii) broadcasts which amount to discussion, argument or opinion on a matter pertaining to religion, belief or conscience; or
(iii) broadcasts which amount to a bona fide discussion, argument or opinion on a matter of public interest.

Children

18. Broadcasters are reminded that children as defined in paragraph 3 above embraces a wide range of maturity and sophistication, and in interpreting this Code it is legitimate for licensees to distinguish, if appropriate those approaching adulthood from a much younger, pre-teenage audience.

18.1 Broadcasters shall not broadcast material unsuitable for children at times when large numbers of children may be expected to be part of the audience.

18.2 Broadcasters shall exercise particular caution, as provided below, in the depiction of violence in children's programming.

18.3 In children's programming portrayed by real-life characters, violence shall, whether physical, verbal or emotional, only be portrayed when it is essential to the development of a character and plot.

18.4 Animated programming for children, while accepted as a stylised form of story-telling which can contain non-realistic violence, shall not have violence as its central theme, and shall not invite dangerous imitation.

18.5 Programming for children shall with due care deal with themes which could threaten their sense of security, when portraying, for example, domestic conflict, death, crime or the use of drugs.

18.6 Programming for children shall with due care deal with themes which could invite children to imitate acts which they see on screen or hear about, such as the use of plastic bags as toys, use of matches, the use of dangerous household products as playthings, or other dangerous physical acts.

18.7 Programming for children shall not contain realistic scenes of violence which create the impression that violence is the preferred or only method to resolve conflict between individuals.

18.8 Programming for children shall not contain realistic scenes of violence which minimise or gloss over the effect of violent acts. Any realistic depictions of violence shall portray, in human terms, the consequences of that violence to its victims and its perpetrators.

18.9 Programming for children shall not contain frightening or otherwise excessive special effects not required by the story line.

Watershed period

19 Programming on television which contains scenes of violence, sexually explicit conduct and/or offensive language intended for adult audiences shall not be broadcast before the watershed period.

20 On the basis that there is a likelihood of older children forming part of the audience during the watershed period, licensees shall adhere to the provisions of Article 32 below (audience advisories) enabling parents to make an informed decision as to the suitability of the programming for their family members.

21 Promotional material and music videos which contain scenes of violence, sexually explicit conduct and/or offensive language intended for adult audiences shall not be broadcast before the watershed period.

22 Some programmes broadcast outside the watershed period will not be suitable for very young children. Licensees should provide sufficient information, in terms of regular scheduling patterns or on-air advice, to assist parents to make appropriate viewing choices.

23 Licensees shall be aware that with the advance of the watershed period progressively less suitable (i.e. more adult) material may be shown and it may be that a programme will be acceptable for example at 23h00 that would not be suitable at 21h00.

24 Broadcasters must be particularly sensitive to the likelihood that programmes which start during the watershed period and which run beyond it may then be viewed by children.

25 Subscription services
    25.1 Where a programme service is only available to viewers on subscription and offers a parental control mechanism, its availability to children may be more restricted and the watershed period may begin at 20h00.

Language

26 Offensive language, including profanity, blasphemy and other religiously insensitive material shall not be used in programmes specially designed for children.

27 No excessively and grossly offensive language should be used before the watershed period on television or at times when large numbers of children are likely to be part of the audience on television or radio. Its use during the periods referred to above should, where practicable, be approved in advance by the licensee's most senior programme executive or the designated alternate.

Sexual conduct

28 Licensees shall not broadcast material, which judged within context, contains a scene or scenes, simulated or real of any of the following:
    (i) A person who is, or is depicted as being under the age of 18 years, participating in, engaging in or assisting another person to engage in sexual conduct or a lewd display of nudity;
    (ii) Explicit violent sexual conduct;
    (iii) Bestiality;
    (iv) Explicit sexual conduct which degrades a person in the sense that it advocates a particular form of hatred based on gender and which constitutes incitement to cause harm; or

29 The prohibition in 28.(i) to 28.(iv) shall not be applicable to bona fide scientific, documentary, dramatic material, which judged within context, is of such a nature. The prohibition in 28.(i), shall however be applicable to artistic material which judged within context, is of such a nature.

30 Scenes depicting sexual conduct, as defined in the Films and Publications Act 65 of 1996, should be broadcast only during the watershed period. Exceptions to this may be allowed in programmes with a serious educational purpose or where the representation is non-explicit and should be approved in advance by the most senior programme executive or a delegated alternate.

31 Explicit portrayal of violent sexual behaviour is justifiable only exceptionally and the same approval process as referred to in 30 above must be followed.

Audience advisories

32 To assist audiences in choosing programmes, licensees shall provide advisory assistance, which when applicable shall include guidelines as to age, at the beginning of broadcasts and wherever necessary, where such broadcasts contain violence, sexual conduct and/or offensive language.

33 Classification

33.1 Where a Film and Publications Board classification exists in terms of the Films and Publications Act No. 65 of 1996 ("Films and Publications Act") for the version of a film or programme intended to be broadcast, such classification certification may be used as a guide for broadcasting.

33.2 No version which has been refused a Film and Publications Board classification certification should be broadcast at any time.

33.3 In all other instances, the provisions of this Code will apply.

34 News

34.1 Licensees shall be obliged to report news truthfully, accurately and fairly.

34.2 News shall be presented in the correct context and in a fair manner, without intentional or negligent departure from the facts, whether by -

(a) Distortion, exaggeration or misrepresentation;

(b) Material omissions; or

(c) Summarisation.

34.3 Only that which may reasonably be true, having due regard to the source of the news, may be presented as fact, and such fact shall be broadcast fairly with due regard to context and importance. Where a report is not based on fact or is founded on opinion, supposition, rumours or allegations, it shall be presented in such manner as to indicate clearly that such is the case.

34.4 Where there is reason to doubt the correctness of the report and it is practicable to verify the correctness thereof, it shall be verified. Where such verification is not practicable, that fact shall be mentioned in the report.

34.5 Where it subsequently appears that a broadcast report was incorrect in a material respect, it shall be rectified forthwith, without reservation or delay. The rectification shall be presented with such a degree of prominence and timing as in the circumstances may be adequate and fair so as to readily attract attention.

34.6 The identity of rape victims and other victims of sexual violence shall not be divulged in any broadcast without the prior consent of the victim concerned.

34.7 Licensees shall advise viewers in advance of scenes or reporting of extraordinary violence, or graphic reporting on delicate subject-matter such as sexual assault or court action related to sexual crimes, particularly during afternoon or early evening newscasts and updates when children would probably be in the audience.

34.8 Licensees shall employ discretion in the use of explicit or graphic language related to stories of destruction, accidents or sexual violence, which could disturb children and sensitive audiences.

35 Comment

35.1 Licensees shall be entitled to broadcast comment on and criticism of any actions or events of public importance.

35.2 Comment shall be an honest expression of opinion and shall be presented in such manner that it appears clearly to be comment, and shall be made on facts truly stated or fairly indicated and referred to.

36 Controversial issues of public importance

36.1 In presenting a programme in which controversial issues of public importance are discussed, a licensee shall make reasonable efforts to fairly present opposing points of view either in the same programme or in a subsequent programme forming part of the same series of programmes presented within a reasonable period of time of the original broadcast and within substantially the same time slot.

36.2 A person whose views are to be criticised in a broadcasting programme on a controversial issue of public importance shall be given a right to reply to such criticism on the same programme. If this is impracticable however, opportunity for response to the programme should be provided where appropriate, for example in a right to reply programme or in a pre-arranged discussion programme with the prior consent of the person concerned.

37 Elections

During any election period, the provisions of sections 58, 59, 60 and 61 of the Act shall apply, and all broadcasting services shall in terms of those sections be subject to the jurisdiction of the Authority.

38 Privacy

Insofar as both news and comment are concerned, broadcasting licensees shall exercise exceptional care and consideration in matters involving the private lives and private concerns of individuals, bearing in mind that the right to privacy may be overridden by a legitimate public interest.

39 Paying a criminal for information

39.1 No payment shall be made to persons involved in crime or other notorious behaviour, or to persons who have been engaged in crime or other notorious behaviour, in order to obtain information concerning any such behaviour, unless compelling societal interests indicate the contrary.

Posted at http://www.icasa.org.za/default.aspx?page=1349

Appendix 2
National Certificate in Journalism

Note: This toolkit has been structured to cover the information needed to acquire the national certificate in journalism, with a special emphasis on radio. The full text of the qualification appears below. But students wanting to specialise in radio should note that they would have to choose the radio-related electives. These are:
• Unit standard 12608: record sound from a single source
• Unit standard 12606: Operate studio equipment for radio production
• Unit standard 12605: Interview and lead discussion for radio broadcast purposes.

Full details of all unit standards required can be found online, at www.saqa.org.za.

SOUTH AFRICAN QUALIFICATIONS AUTHORITY
REGISTERED QUALIFICATION:

National Certificate: Journalism

SAQA QUAL ID	QUALIFICATION TITLE	
49123	National Certificate: Journalism	
SGB NAME	**NSB**	**REGISTERING PROVIDER**
SGB Journalism	NSB 04-Communication Studies and Language	
Quality Assuring ETQA		
MAPPP-Media, Advertising, Publishing, Printing and Packaging		
QUALIFICATION TYPE	**FIELD**	**SUBFIELD**
National Higher Certificate	Communication Studies and Language	Information Studies
ABET BAND	**MINIMUM CREDITS**	**NQF LEVEL**	**QUAL CLASS**
Undefined	120	Level 5	Regular-Unit Stds Based
REGISTRATION STATUS	**SAQA DECISION NUMBER**	**REGISTRATION START DATE**	**REGISTRATION END DATE**
Registered	SAQA 0657/04	2004-12-02	2007-12-02

Purpose and rationale of the qualification

This qualification has been developed for people who work or intend to work as junior journalists and who seek recognition for essential competence. Recipients of this qualification are able to write a variety of journalism texts and report at entry level. The qualification is designed to be flexible and accessible to all in journalism and wishing to enter journalism after undergraduate study or equivalent experience. It allows people to write and report in accordance with the requirements of a specific media news enterprise. The core competencies lay the foundation for a person to develop a career in sub-editing, writing and/or reporting. The elective category makes provision for specialisation in a particular medium or section of a medium and entry into sub-editing, and in doing so, increases the learner's employment possibilities.

The qualification aims to provide a bridge into the industry. Learners who qualify can be employed as junior journalists. They gather information from all media such as television, radio and newspapers, generate story ideas to present to news editors, receive and interact with story briefs, organise themselves going after stories, research backgrounds, make appointments and see people, observe, interview, judge news value, evaluate information, communicate, keep to strict deadlines, debrief, inform others, conduct follow-up meetings, develop story plans, write stories, check contexts and gaps in information, send stories to news editors, and follow-up their stories with the news editor, and plan. Competent junior journalists must be able to interact with other reporters, respect roles, have newsgathering instincts, and an insatiable curiosity.

On achieving this qualification learners are capable of: .
• Collecting information for journalistic purposes
• Reporting for a variety of general journalistic purposes
• Writing stories for a variety of journalistic purposes
• Interviewing for a variety of general journalistic purposes
• Performing journalism related tasks in an editorial environment
• Employing work-related stress management strategies
• Improving their own performance
• Presenting story ideas
• Describing the implications of democracy for a diverse society
• Contributing to information distribution regarding HIV/AIDS

In addition, qualified learners choose to become capable of:
• Sub-editing, for two specialist beats OR
• Reporting, for a specialist beat, in two mediums OR
• Communicating proficiently in a second language as a junior journalist

Rationale

This qualification has been developed for professional practice across the media industry and is intended to professionalise junior journalists, ensuring the upliftment of the standards in general and the image of journalism. It is applicable to small and large organisations alike. The qualification is aimed at aspirant journalists. Generally, learners have already attained a first qualification, such as a diploma or degree (NQF Level 5 or 6) in any area of specialisation prior to attempting this qualification, and experience as a journalist should be evaluated for recognition of prior learning. Qualified learners will be employable as junior journalists, in print, radio, television, etc.

Media organisations require a diversity of journalists but past legacies have prevented this from occurring. Sub-editing skills are currently not given sufficient emphasis or focus in existing journalism qualifications. There is a need for a qualification that recognises this skill area of journalism. It will encourage learners to pursue this particular career path in journalism and give recognition to people who are currently working as journalists and sub-editors but do not have formal qualifications recognising their competence.

In recent times, the media have been accused of racism and recommendations were made to address the issue through formal and non-formal training, and recruitment of black staff, especially sub-editors and journalists who have an understanding of democratic institutions and human rights (SAHRC: Faultlines, August 2000). There is a need for establishing entry-level programmes for aspirant journalists, including addressing issues of professional standards and ethics, and understanding of the Constitution and human rights.

Qualified learners can progress to specialist journalism beats and higher levels of journalistic competence and editorial management. In addition, the inclusion of transferable competence in this qualification allows them to pursue other careers such as academia, graphic design, HTML editing, general management, human resource management, media law, and policy-making. This qualification is aimed at enhancing employability, effective operation in a business or operational environment, producing usable content and products for specific outlets. Improved journalistic competence will result in increased accuracy of information, improved informed public opinion, an improved educated public, and more reliable information, so that people can make a contribution to the South African democracy as citizens. The competencies attained to qualify will contribute towards responsible journalism, freedom of expression, access to information, credibility for the profession, and ethical journalism. Competent journalists can encourage investment, improve economic literacy, and information flow about business and investments, and can improve the saleability of media products to improve the success of the sector. After the King III report, journalists also play an important role in corporate governance, through non-financial reporting.

Learning assumed to be in place and recognition of prior learning

This qualification was designed and credited based on the assumption that a learner entering a programme leading to this qualification has achieved a Certificate or Diploma at NQF level 5 for a baseline of general knowledge in a particular area of interest to the learner, such as politics, sport, or education, or equivalent and has communication and language competence in one language at NQF Level 4. In addition, it is assumed that learners understand sexuality and sexually transmitted infections including HIV/AIDS (NLRD

ID Nr 14656). Assumed to be in place are communication and language competencies in one language at NQF level 5, and another language at NQF level 3, and mathematic literacy at NQF Level 4. It also assumes that the following computer literacy competencies have been attained:

- Demonstrate the ability to use electronic mail software to send and receive messages (NLRD ID Nr 7571)
- Demonstrate knowledge of and produce word processing documents using basic functions (NLRD ID Nr 7568)
- Demonstrate ability to use the World Wide Web (NLRD ID Nr 7573)

This qualification will not be awarded if these computer literacy competencies are not in place.

Recognition of prior learning (RPL)

This qualification can be achieved wholly, or in part, through recognition of prior learning. Evidence can be presented in a variety of forms, including previous international or local qualifications, reports, testimonials, mentoring, functions performed, portfolios, work records and performance records. As such, evidence should be judged according to the general principles of assessment described in the notes to assessors below. Learners who have met the requirements of any Unit Standard that forms part of this qualification may apply for recognition of prior learning to the relevant Education and Training Quality Assurance body (ETQA). The applicant must be assessed against the specific outcomes and with the assessment criteria for the relevant Unit Standards. A qualification will be awarded should a learner demonstrate that the exit level outcomes of the qualification have been attained.

Recognise previous learning?

Y

Qualification rules

The Fundamental Component Unit Standards are compulsory (6 credits). All the Core Component Unit Standards are compulsory (74 credits). For the Elective Component learners are required to attain between 40 and 50 credits. The following options are available for the Elective Component:

1. Language and communication in a second language (at NQF Level 4) (20 credits) and 20 credits from other sectors OR
2. Sub-editing, including two specialist beats, and layout and design of print media (35 credits) and 10 credits from other sectors OR
3. Reporting, for an additional medium in a specialist beat, recording sound and interviewing for radio (33 credits) and 10 credits from other sectors.

Exit level outcomes

Fundamental and Core

1. Communicate effectively with interview subjects, sources, the public, and teams
2. Work in a team to meet given time frames and contribute to effective working relations in teams
3. Research a variety of topics, events and issues to produce relevant information and verify sources for facts used
4. Report ethically and professionally to record and produce facts and descriptions
5. Produce final form output that uses language and idiom correctly and appropriately for specified contexts
6. Time and other resources are managed to consistently meet given production deadlines
7. Evaluate journalistic conduct and output - Range: this does not include writing analysis pieces

Elective (one is required to qualify)

1. Sub-edit general text that cover two specialist beats
2. Report regarding a specialist beat and in a second medium
3. Communicate effectively using language skills in the mode of written presentation in a second language

Associated assessment criteria

Fundamental and Core

1.
• Information produced is relevant for specified contexts
• Communication is clear, unambiguous, understandable, focused, direct and complete
• Communication is regular
• Communication format is relevant for contexts and purpose
• Communication allows for feedback
• Questions are appropriate for contexts to require and clarify information
• Identification of criteria for relevance of information is correct
2.
• Information sharing is continuous and appropriate for given goals, objectives, and roles of specific teams
• Description of team roles is accurate
• Input from others is sought and encouraged
• Assistance offered is appropriate for specific needs, and in a manner appropriate for the working style of specific teams
3.
• Legal requirements are adhered to

- Sources used are credible

Range: sources include primary and verification sources

- Sources are relevant for information needs
- Research processes used meet agreed principles of fairness and diversity
- Information gathering methodologies are relevant for information needs
- Information gathered is verifiable and contributes to story and reporting planning and contexts
- Records kept are accessible and meet specified requirements and conventions

4.

- Facts and descriptions are accurate, reveals information and contributes to the public's understanding of stories covered
- Reporting plans are informed by research findings
- Preparation is appropriate for specified contexts
- Reporting is factually accurate
- Observations are noted as such in forms appropriate for specified contexts
- Reporting meets specified criteria for relevance within specific contexts
- Agreed ethical and professional requirements are adhered to at all times
- Legal requirements are adhered to

5.

- Legal requirements are adhered to
- Final form outputs are justified in terms of appeal to intended recipients
- Final form outputs enhance public understanding of events, issues or topics
- Language and idiom meets specified style and format requirements
- Form and format meet specified style and format requirements
- Facts are verified where relevant and/or required
- Final form outputs meet specified criteria for relevance within specific contexts

6.

- Planning is feasible in terms of given time requirements
- Methods selected are justified in terms of time and resource constraints
- All relevant deadlines are identified
- Communication is timeous
- Own contributions to teams are scheduled to meet given deadlines, and do not impact negatively on other team members
- Reporting meets given deadlines
- Technology is used appropriately and securely
- Relevant safety, health, environment, security and operational requirements are adhered to

7.

- Legal, professional and ethical requirements are adhered to
- Criteria used for evaluation of journalistic conduct and output are relevant for specific contexts
- Evaluation findings and choices are justified in terms of specified legal, professional and ethical requirements

Elective (one is required to qualify)

1.
• Relevant protocols of two specialist beats are adhered to
• Writing for two specialist beats is accurate
• Writing for two specialist beats is comprehensive in terms of specified requirements and
  contexts
Range: people, events, proceeding, findings, topics and issues related to the specialist
beats are included
• Sub-editing reflects specified requirements of given contexts
Range: requirements can include, style, length of text, language use, structure, headlines,
  layout, etc.
• Content of text is accurate and verified
• Interpretation of design messages is justified in terms of agreed design elements and
  principles
• Assessment of the quality of own and other`s writing is justified in terms of specified
  requirements
• Feedback to and coaching of others meets specified requirements
2.
• Relevant protocols of a specialist beat are adhered to
• Writing for a specialist beat is accurate
• Writing for a specialist beat is comprehensive in terms of specified requirements and
  contexts
Range: people, events, proceeding, findings, topics and issues related to the specialist
beat are included
• Recorded sound quality during interviews is sufficient for reference purposes
  afterwards
• Preparation meets specified context requirements
Range: requirements can include specifications for stories, resources, sources, etc.
• Information selected is appropriate for purpose and context
• Reporting and recording of information meets specified context and legal requirements
Range: requirements can include various methods and techniques for information
gathering, accurate information, principles of balance, diversity and fairness, etc
3.
• Text types, text features and text functions are correctly identified, selected and verified
  in relation to parallel texts
• Texts are design based on context-specific requirements
• The writing process is planned effectively
• Errors in text are accurately identified and analysed
• Feedback regarding text is obtained and provided
• Linguistic or textual features are accurately assessed
• Text assessment findings are justified
• Strategies selected to improve and transform text are context-appropriate and justified
• Comparison of own composition with similar text types is relevant

- Text quality is improved where relevant
- Adaptations of text for different readerships is appropriate for specific readership profiles
- The conceptual level of text is adjusted to correct readership level.

Integrated assessment

The assessment criteria in the unit standards are performance-based, assessing applied competence rather than only knowledge, or skills. In addition, learners must demonstrate that they can achieve the outcomes in an integrated manner, dealing effectively with different and random demands related to the environmental conditions in occupational contexts, to qualify. Evidence is required that the learner is able to achieve the exit level outcomes of the qualification as a whole and thus its purpose, at the time of the award of the qualification. Workplace experience can be recognised when assessing towards this qualification.

Integrated assessment provides learners with an opportunity to display an ability to integrate practical performance, actions, concepts and theory across unit standards to achieve competence in relation to the purpose of this qualification. Before qualifying, the learner will be expected to demonstrate competence that integrates all specific outcomes, for all Unit Standards, for example, applying competence in a practical scenario. In addition, during the learning process to attain the outcomes of each Unit Standard, learners will be expected to give evidence that they have attained the embedded knowledge and specific skills contained in specific outcomes for the relevant Unit Standard.

International comparability

Journalists can receive their entry-level training in-service (while employed), and most training happens after a learner attains a first qualification. In Uganda, journalists attain a degree in mass communication/journalism, or a degree in another discipline followed by a journalism diploma. Requirements in Sierra-Leone are that a university degree and four years` experience in journalism is equivalent of a qualification in journalism. Similarly, in Yemen, entry-level journalists are required to have a qualification from a college or institute, or have journalistic experience of not less than three years.

In New Zealand, Journalism is classified as part of the community and social services field. Three qualifications exist, including the National Diploma in Journalism with strands in Magazine, Newspaper, Radio, and Television. Notably, the biggest differences between this qualification and the South African one is the presence of streams for each medium in the New Zealand qualification, and the fact that it is at a level lower. Credits are comparable, and the following competencies are addressed in the New Zealand qualification, but not in the South African qualification: reporting the local government sector; using shorthand for journalism; reporting Treaty of Waitangi issues; investigating how different cultural viewpoints are expressed in the media; and taking and selecting news photos. There is only a three-year Diploma in New Zealand that is at a level equivalent to South African NQF Level 5.

The qualifications in Pakistan do not achieve what this South African qualification achieves. Most of the training in Pakistan does not include the use of the Internet for information gathering, or web-based publishing, as most institutions do not have Internet facilities. Most learning takes place informally with the competence of most journalists based also on the willingness (and competence) of senior employees in the media organisations. There is little cooperation between institutions, resulting in an undefined and variable national standard.

In Holland, journalism qualifications are generally much longer than this South African qualification (up to four years for an entry-level journalism qualification) and start at degree level. However, an exit point is generally available after one year, and is slightly less complex than the South African qualification. Included are typically the following learning components:

• Introduction to the professional practice, including current affairs, meetings and discussion with professional journalists, and introduction to the various professions
• Mass communication
• Geography, town and country planning, environment
• Contemporary history
• Statistics
• Economics
• Political science and constitutional history
• Communication and of language
• Development of English writing skills (news items, press releases)
• Development of editorial skills (selecting and ordering)
• Word processing techniques

In the United Kingdom, the only qualification registered on the framework is that of Broadcast Journalism. The qualification is more complex than the South African certificate, and addresses primarily editorial management competence. Nonetheless, various programs are available for journalism. The closest equivalent for this South African qualification is the Higher National Certificate (National Council for the Training of Journalists), considered to be a pre-entry qualification, based on the assumption that a learner has already attained a degree in another discipline. This qualification includes:

• Writing skills
• Research and interview techniques
• Law
• Shorthand
• Public affairs/administration
• Word processing
• Production and design
• Sub-editing

Electives include feature writing, radio news journalism, desktop publishing techniques, editorial graphic art, editing, and proof reading. Programs are generally context-specific (e.g. newspaper journalism, magazine journalism, or graphics journalism) and duration varies from 20 weeks (6 months) to a year.

Most employers in the United States of America prefer individuals with a bachelor's degree in journalism. However, journalism training starts at high school (South African Further Education and Training level equivalent), with mentorship options at some schools. Most qualifications in Journalism are graduate programs (a level above this South African certificate), with specialisations. There are no competencies in the American qualifications that are not addressed here albeit probably at a lower level of complexity.

Canadian education and training of journalists include pre-graduate modules from second year (NQF 5 and 6 equivalent), as well as post graduate diplomas aimed at learners with degrees in other disciplines, that are equivalent to components of this South African qualification. Aspects that differ most from the South African qualification include Broadcast Public Affairs (3 credits), and the fact that ethics is covered much later in the program, falling outside the equivalent for the South African qualification.

In Australia, a Graduate Certificate of Journalism (6 months) exists. However, the Graduate Diploma of Journalism (one year) is the equivalent of this qualification. The qualification requires a first degree at entry. Competence included in the core is the equivalent of this South African qualification, and electives in the Australian qualification include professional writing, literary studies, children's literature, media and communication, public relations, etc.

In Tanzania various professional and 'sub professional' qualifications in journalism offered. There an equivalent of this South African qualification, namely, a one-year certificate programme. Tanzania also has post-graduate diploma courses (generally two years), intermediate certificate courses, advanced certificate courses, and advanced diploma courses (up to 3 years of learning) with some overlap with the South African qualification. Also, short courses offered include courses about news writing, public relations, mass communication, and broadcasting, a 1 to 3 month basic certificate in journalism and short courses in social ethics, press law, gender issues and development studies.

Articulation options

The qualification builds on other certificates, diplomas and degrees at NQF Level 5 and 6, from a range of sub-sectors and provides articulation with a range of qualifications in communications, media studies and journalism, such as:

_ First degrees in Journalism, at NQF Level 6
_ First degree in Design, at NQF Level 6
_ National Diploma in Translation, at NQF Level 5
_ National Certificate in Television Operations, at NQF Level 5
_ National Certificate in Radio Production, at NQF Level 5

Moderation options

Moderation of assessment and accreditation of providers shall be at the discretion of a relevant ETQA as long as it complies with the SAQA requirements. The ETQA is responsible for moderation of learner achievements of learners who meet the requirements of this qualification. Particular moderation and accreditation requirements are:

- Any institution offering learning that will enable the achievement of this qualification must be accredited as a provider with the relevant ETQA. Providers offering learning towards achievement of any of the unit standards that make up this qualification must also be accredited through the relevant ETQA accredited by SAQA.
- The ETQA will oversee assessment and moderation of assessment according to their policies and guidelines for assessment and moderation, or in terms of agreements reached around assessment and moderation between the relevant ETQA and other ETQAs and in terms of the moderation guideline detailed here.
- Moderation must include both internal and external moderation of assessments for the qualification, unless the relevant ETQA policies specify otherwise. Moderation should also encompass achievement of the competence described in Unit Standards as well as the integrated competence described in the qualification.
- Internal moderation of assessment must take place at the point of assessment with external moderation provided by a relevant ETQA according to the moderation guidelines and the agreed ETQA procedures.
- Anyone wishing to be assessed against this qualification may apply to be assessed by any assessment agency, assessor or provider institution that is accredited by the relevant ETQA.

Criteria for the registration of assessors

Assessment of learner achievements takes place at providers accredited by the relevant ETQA (RSA, 1998b) for the provision of programs that result in the outcomes specified for this qualification. Anyone assessing a learner or moderating the assessment of a learner against this qualification must be registered as an assessor with the ETQA. Assessors registered with the relevant ETQA must carry out the assessment of learners for the qualification and any of the Unit Standards that make up this qualification.

To register as an assessor, the following are required:
- Detailed documentary proof of relevant qualification/s, practical training completed, and experience gained, at a level above the level of this qualification
- NQF recognised assessor credit

Assessors should keep the following general principles in mind when designing and conducting assessments:
- Focus the initial assessment activities on gathering evidence in terms of the main outcomes expressed in the titles of the Unit Standards to ensure assessment is integrated

rather than fragmented. Remember that the learner needs to be declared competent in terms of the qualification purpose and exit level outcomes.
• Where assessment across Unit Standard titles or at Unit Standard title level is unmanageable, then focus assessment around each specific outcome, or groups of specific outcomes. Take special note of the need for integrated assessment.
• Make sure evidence is gathered across the entire range, wherever it applies.

In particular, assessors should assess that the learner demonstrates an ability to consider a range of options by:
• Measuring the quality of the observed practical performance as well as the theory and underpinning knowledge.
• Using methods that are varied to allow the learner to display thinking and decision making in the demonstration of practical performance.
• Maintaining a balance between practical performance and theoretical assessment methods to ensure each is measured in accordance with the level of the qualification.
• Taking into account that the relationship between practical and theoretical components is not fixed, but varies according to the type and level of qualification.

All assessments should be conducted in line with the following well-documented principles:
Appropriate: The method of assessment is suited to the performance being assessed.
• Fair: The method of assessment does not present any barriers to achievements, which are not related to the evidence.
• Manageable: The methods used make for easily arranged cost-effective assessments that do not unduly interfere with learning.
• Integrate into work or learning: Evidence collection is integrated into the work or learning process where this is appropriate and feasible.
• Valid: The assessment focuses on the requirements laid down in the standards; i.e. the assessment is fit for purpose.
• Direct: The activities in the assessment mirror the conditions of actual performance as close as possible.
• Authentic: The assessor is satisfied that the work being assessed is attributable to the learner being assessed.
• Sufficient: The evidence collected establishes that all criteria have been met and that performance to the required Standard can be repeated consistently.
• Systematic: Planning and recording is sufficiently rigorous to ensure that assessment is fair.
• Open: Learners can contribute to the planning and accumulation of evidence. Learners for assessment understand the assessment process and the criteria that apply.
• Consistent: The same assessor would make the same judgement again in similar circumstances. The judgement made is similar than the judgement that would be made by other assessors

Notes

N/A

Unit standards:

	ID	UNIT STANDARD TITLE	LEVEL	CREDITS
Core	8555	Contribute to information distribution regarding HIV/AIDS in the workplace	Level 4	4
Core	15096	Demonstrate an understanding of stress in order to apply strategies to achieve optimal stress levels in personal and work situations	Level 5	5
Core	15093	Demonstrate insight into democracy as a form of governance and its implications for a diverse society	Level 5	5
Core	110360	Interview for a variety of journalistic purposes	Level 5	8
Core	11994	Monitor, reflect and improve on own performance	Level 5	3
Core	110359	Perform journalism-related tasks and generate journalistic material in an editorial environment	Level 5	20
Core	117545	Present journalistic story ideas	Level 5	5
Core	110357	Report for a variety of journalistic purposes	Level 5	12
Core	110361	Write stories for a variety of journalistic purposes in print	Level 6	12
Funda-mental	117546	Collect information for journalistic use	Level 5	6
Elective	114600	Apply innovative thinking to the development of a small business	Level 4	4
Elective	114742	Calculate tax payable by a small business	Level 4	6
Elective	117241	Develop a business plan for a small business	Level 4	5
Elective	8974	Engage in sustained oral communication and evaluate spoken texts	Level 4	5
Elective	117244	Investigate the possibilities of establishing and running a small business enterprise (SMME)	Level 4	3
Elective	114738	Perform financial planning and control functions for a small business	Level 4	6
Elective	8975	Read analyse and respond to a variety of texts	Level 4	5
Elective	12608	Record sound from a single source	Level 4	3
Elective	12153	Use the writing process to compose texts required in the business environment	Level 4	5

	ID	UNIT STANDARD TITLE	LEVEL	CREDITS
Elective	8976	Write for a wide range of contexts	Level 4	5
Elective	15234	Apply efficient time management to the work of a department/division/section	Level 5	4
Elective	8647	Apply workplace communication skills	Level 5	10
Elective	117539	Assess the quality of written text	Level 5	5
Elective	15237	Build teams to meet set goals and objectives	Level 5	3
Elective	117541	Cover a specialist beat as a journalist	Level 5	6
Elective	15231	Create and use a range of resources to effectively manage teams, sections, departments or divisions	Level 5	4
Elective	15216	Create opportunities for innovation and lead projects to meet innovative ideas	Level 5	4
Elective	15219	Develop and implement a strategy and action plans for a team, department or division	Level 5	4
Elective	10043	Develop, implement and manage a project / activity plan	Level 5	5
Elective	114481	Develop, maintain and monitor media relations to communicate government information	Level 5	5
Elective	15238	Devise and apply strategies to establish and maintain relationships	Level 5	3
Elective	15224	Empower team members through recognising strengths, encouraging participation in decision making and delegating tasks	Level 5	4
Elective	15233	Harness diversity and build on strengths of a diverse working environment	Level 5	3
Elective	15225	Identify and interpret related legislation and its impact on the team, department or division and ensure compliance	Level 5	4
Elective	15229	Implement codes of conduct in the team, department or division	Level 5	3
Elective	15230	Monitor team members and measure effectiveness of performance	Level 5	4
Elective	12606	Operate studio equipment for radio production	Level 5	5
Elective	14525	Present an informed argument on a current issue in a business sector	Level 5	5
Elective	15214	Recognise areas in need of change, make recommendations and implement change in the team, department or division	Level 5	3
Elective	110358	Sub-edit non-specialist text	Level 5	10
Elective	12605	Interview and lead discussion for radio broadcast purposes	Level 6	12

	ID	UNIT STANDARD TITLE	LEVEL	CREDITS
Elective	115020	Use standardised technical language	Level 6	10
Elective	115081	Write technical text within a specific field	Level 6	10
Elective	117945	Design documents	Level 7	20

Source: SA Qualifications Authority

Appendix 3
Template for 10-day course

Note: This template is intended as a basis for trainers to develop their own courses. It does not aim to be a fully fleshed out course. Training should be designed specifically for the audience, taking into account level of skill, facilities, the size of the group and much else. This template is only intended as a rough guide, to help get the trainer started on planning.

The template is based on a training day of three two-hour sessions. For simplicity's sake, all sessions have been kept to the same length, although it is probably desirable to tailor the actual timeslots much more closely to the content. Some may need to be longer, and some shorter.

You may want to build in additional elements, like a daily review of the learning gone through on the day before.

The template assumes that the group will have access to field recorders and studio editing facilities.

Day	Session	Agenda	Notes for trainer	Exercises	Toolkit ref
Mon	1	Introduction	Introduce participants and course, sort out expectations, set groundrules. An icebreaker is useful.		
	2	The radio landscape	Talk through Ch 1: Radio as a medium; different kinds of radio stations; legal framework.	Do it! box in Ch 1	Ch 1
	3	News values game	Use exercise 2 in the Do it! Box in Ch 2: split group into smaller groups, and have them come up with a running order. Develop a discussion around news values out of that exercise.	Ex 2 in the Do it! Box in Ch 2.	Ch 2
Tues	1	Radio & journalism: roles & formats	Talk through the structure of newsrooms, and the formats of radio news.		pp

Day	Session	Agenda	Notes for trainer	Exercises	Toolkit ref
	2	Generating ideas	Talk through the beginning of Ch 3. Then have small groups generate ideas	Exercises 1 & 2 in Do it box, Ch 3	Ch 3
	3	Research	Talk through "getting the information" in Ch 3, then do the exercise	Do it! box in Ch 3	Ch 3
Wed	1	Production values	Play a radio bulletin, and discuss what works and what does not. Generate a discussion about what makes good radio, and list those production values on a flipchart or board		Ch 6
	2	Writing for radio	Talk through Ch 4		Ch 4
	3	Writing for radio - practical	Get people to write bulletin stories. Crit each other's stories	Do it! box in Ch 4	
Thur	1	Recording sound - theory and practical	Introduce the field recorder. Have people interview each other. Try to include different settings, so they have to cope with different background sound. Listen back to the results, and discuss them.	Do it! box in Ch 5	Ch 5
	2	Recording sound cont	Continue exercise		
	3	Visit to newsroom	Arrange a visit to a newsroom, so that the participants can see what it looks like and meet some reporters.		
Fri	1	Bulletin exercise	Talk through Ch 10. Divide into groups to compile a five-minute bulletin. If possible, it is good to have people work on real stories, but this would probably have to be set up early in the week to	Do it! box in Ch 10	Ch 10

Day	Session	Agenda	Notes for trainer	Exercises	Toolkit ref
			allow people to research them. Otherwise, you can also use fictional stories.		
	2	Bulletin exercise cont	Continue exercise. Finish with debriefing.		
	3	Law & ethics	Talk through Ch 13. Then discuss some scenarios.	Do it! box in Ch 13	Ch 13
Mon	1	Digital editing	Introduce group to basic functions of audio editing software. Spend the rest of the day cutting sound, editing interviews and getting generally familiar with the technology.	Do it! box in Ch 8 Use sound on CD	Ch 8
	2	Digital editing continued			
	3	Digital editing continued			
Tues	1	Packaging	Talk through Ch 9. Listen to some examples of good packages, and discuss what makes them good.	Do it! box in Ch 9	Ch 9
	2	Current affairs shows	Talk through Ch 11. Listen to a segment of a good current affairs show, and discuss what works and what doesn't.	Do it! box in Ch 11	Ch 11
	3	Plan show	Lead into planning of a show the group will produce on the last day. It is best not to attempt too much - no more than 20 - 30 mins. Try to make sure the show includes various formats, including interviews, packages and a short discussion. It is possible to design a show around a particular appropriate theme. Give the show a name.		

Day	Session	Agenda	Notes for trainer	Exercises	Toolkit ref
Wed	1	Practical work for show	The group needs to gather, write up and edit the material for Friday. Running orders need to be drawn up, if possible a jingle. The facilitator should be available to work with individuals throughout this time, to deepen skills. A field trip could be arranged during this time, or somebody could be asked to come in and address the group, who would then write up stories resulting from the input. During this time, individuals should also be given an opportunity to practice presentation skills		
	2	.. cont			
	3	.. cont			
Thur	1	.. cont			
	2	.. cont			
	3	.. cont			
Fri	1	Current affairs show	The course show goes to air! It is important to stick to deadlines, to give people the feeling of doing real radio.		
	2	Debrief of show	Plenary discussion: what went wrong? What went right?		
	3	Review of course	It's important to finish with a summary, and allow participants to evaluate the course.		